The Work Sampling System®

Using Work Sampling Guidelines and Checklists

An Observational Assessment

PEARSON

www.PearsonSchool.com

The Work Sampling Observational Assessment enables teachers to monitor children's academic, social, emotional, and physical progress by observing, recording, and evaluating student learning. It is based on teachers' careful observations of students' classroom performance and progress and is designed to provide meaningful feedback to teachers, students, families, and administrators. The Work Sampling Observational Assessment helps teachers make instructional decisions based on information about individual students and helps teachers better understand what they should be teaching, what children have to master, and what children are having difficulty learning.

Using Work Sampling Guidelines and Checklists

An Observational Assessment

Margo L. Dichtelmiller
Judy R. Jablon
Samuel J. Meisels
Dorothea B. Marsden
Aviva B. Dorfman

The Work Sampling System®

Pearson Education, Inc.

For more information about
The Work Sampling System:

call 1-800-321-3106

www.pearsonschool.com

Development of The Work Sampling System was supported in part by a grant from the John D. and Catherine T. MacArthur Foundation. The opinions expressed are solely those of the authors.

Material in this book is derived in part from *Work Sampling in the Classroom: A Teacher's Manual.*

Printed in the United States of America
4 5 6 7 8   11 10 09 08 07

ISBN 1-57212-261-7

List of Frequently Asked Questions

How to Use this Book

Introduction

This book is written for teachers who want a systematic way to gather information about their students' learning, classroom performance, and academic progress. It describes an observational assessment that uses the Work Sampling Developmental Guidelines and Checklists to monitor student performance in an ongoing manner. This approach can be used by an individual teacher who wishes to keep track of what her students are learning and how well they are learning it. It can also be used by a group of teachers or an entire school or program to enhance the consistency of instruction and to improve assessment practices across classrooms.

The Work Sampling Developmental Guidelines and Checklists are part of the **Work Sampling System,** an authentic performance assessment for children from three years of age through fifth grade. The purpose of the Work Sampling System is to document and assess children's skills, knowledge, behavior, and accomplishments across a wide variety of curriculum areas on multiple occasions in order to enhance teaching and learning.

The Work Sampling System consists of three complementary elements:

1) Developmental Guidelines and Checklists
2) Portfolios, and
3) Summary Reports

The Work Sampling System calls for ongoing assessment that is summarized three times per year. By reflecting classroom goals and objectives, it helps teachers monitor children's continuous progress and places children's work within a broad developmental perspective. Through documenting and evaluating individual performance of classroom-based tasks, the Work Sampling System strengthens student motivation, assists teachers in instructional decision-making, and serves as an effective means for reporting children's progress to families, educators, and the community.

Organization of this Book

This book is divided into six chapters and two appendixes. Chapter 1 briefly describes observational assessment and curriculum-embedded performance assessment. It also suggests a plan for individual teachers or school-wide groups of teachers to get started observing in a focused way by using the Work Sampling Guidelines and Checklists. Chapter 2 describes the Developmental Guidelines and Checklists, beginning with a one-page overview of their primary features, followed by an explanation of their purposes and structure, and a discussion of important concepts and terminology. Chapter 3 describes how to use Guidelines and Checklists. It contains a timeline, and describes what teachers must do before the school year begins, during each reporting period, and near the end of each reporting period in order to use Guidelines and Checklists successfully. Chapter 4 uses a question/answer format to address specific issues that have been raised by teachers who have used the Work Sampling Guidelines and Checklists in the past. Chapter 5 discusses reporting methods that complement this type of observational assessment and suggests several different options that can be used. The final chapter focuses on specific uses of Guidelines and Checklists for different classroom settings: preschool and kindergarten, older elementary, multi-age classrooms, Title I, and special needs.

Using this Book

This book can be approached in several different ways. If you want to begin immediately to observe and use the Work Sampling Guidelines and Checklists, read Chapter 2 for an overview and introduction, and then proceed to Chapter 3 for "how to" instructions. As you read Chapter 3, take one section at a time. After you read a section, give yourself some time to implement what you have read. Go through the first sections, "Guidelines and Checklists Timeline" and "Before the School Year Begins," and then take some time to study the Guidelines, prepare some observation tools that you are likely to use, and set up an organization system to store your observational records and Checklists. Once you have a working knowledge of that section, go on to read "During Each Reporting Period" and actually begin to observe and use the Checklists. After you have observed for a month or two, read the section called "Near the End of Each Reporting Period" and get ready to summarize what you know about your students from this period of observation. Throughout this process, when you have questions, check the list of Frequently Asked

Questions in Chapter 4 for answers to your questions.

Some teachers like to read the entire manual, study the Guidelines, and then set up a schedule of tasks to complete, referring back to the manual regularly as they approach each new activity. In Chapter 1, we have prepared a list of steps to get you started observing and using the Checklists.

Getting in Touch

If you have questions, or would like information about other Work Sampling products, we can be found on the Web at www.pearsonschool.com. Feel free to call for information about products or training at 1-800-321-3106.

Chapter 1

Getting Started with Observational Assessment

THE WORK SAMPLING DEVELOPMENTAL GUIDELINES AND Checklists is a classroom-based observational *performance assessment**. Its purpose is to help teachers document and evaluate children's skills, knowledge, and behaviors using actual classroom experiences, activities, and products. The primary assessment method is focused observation. As students solve mathematical problems, write in journals, construct with blocks, paint, engage in scientific experimentation, or simply interact with their peers, teachers can observe, record their observations, and use these observations to evaluate student learning.

All performance assessments rely on students to demonstrate specific skills and competencies and to apply the skills and knowledge they have mastered. The Work Sampling Guidelines and Checklists are based on the premise that children are active constructors of knowledge who are capable of analyzing, synthesizing, evaluating, and interpreting facts and ideas. "Authentic" performance assessment focuses on observing and recording what the student is learning in a "real-life" context—one in which students perform chosen tasks as they would in the process of general instruction.

Observational assessment with the Work Sampling Guidelines and Checklists is also known as *"curriculum-embedded"* assessment. This means that teachers assess student learning as students engage in ongoing classroom activities. The assessment activities are embedded within regular, ongoing classroom curriculum activities; they are not introduced from outside the classroom. This approach is very sensitive to classroom

---

*See the Glossary in Appendix A for definition of terms shown in **bold italics**.

context, recognizing that teachers differ in their approaches to teaching, just as learners differ in the ways they learn. Therefore, this approach does not dictate curriculum or instructional methods. Instead, it is designed to be used with a wide variety of curricula, with diverse groups of students, and in a wide variety of settings.

The Work Sampling Guidelines and Checklists go well beyond many performance assessments that try to assess student competence by exposing children to "on-demand" performance tasks in which choices are severely restricted for both students and teachers. With this assessment, competence is not assessed on the basis of a single performance; rather, a student's performance is assessed repeatedly as it occurs naturally in the classroom. Over time and in the context of numerous performances, teachers can observe the patterns of student learning—what students' strengths are, and where their weaker areas might be. These patterns constitute the evidence on which the assessment is based. Comparisons between students are minimized, since students are evaluated according to how well their level of performance conforms to the standards on which the Guidelines are based.

The Work Sampling Guidelines and Checklists is primarily an instructional assessment designed to help teachers make informed instructional decisions in their classrooms. When teachers have reliable information about their students' learning and accomplishments, they are able to understand children's behavior, address areas of weakness, and individualize instruction to help each child reach his or her potential. The Work Sampling Guidelines and Checklists enable teachers to follow children's development over time and within and across domains, in order to create rich profiles of children's accomplishments and approaches to learning.

Steps for Getting Started

Depending on your experience as a classroom observer, you may elect to begin by focusing on several domains or by using all domains from the beginning. If you are very comfortable observing and recording your observations, it is likely that after a review of the Guidelines, you can begin using all seven curriculum domains included in Work Sampling. However, if systematic observation is new to you, you might decide to focus on two to four domains at first, while you organize and practice focused observation.

We suggest the following steps as a way to learn to use the Developmental Guidelines and Checklists to assess your students:

1 Read and become familiar with the Developmental Guidelines (p. 18).

2 Think about how, when, and what you want to observe (p. 20).

3 Set up an organization system for observation and Checklist review (p. 23). Create a teacher file to store:

- the Checklist
- notes and reminders about activities to observe or plan
- observation notes
- correspondence with the family
- any other material about children that will help you evaluate their learning

4 Decide on the methods and tools you will use for documenting your observations of children (p. 26).

- Select any of the Checklist Process Notes that seem useful to you (see Chapter 3).
- Make enough copies of your process notes to use during the first weeks of school.
- If you prefer other ways of recording your observations, design a master for duplication or prepare the materials for use.
- Fill in your students' names as appropriate on the observational materials.

5 Develop a plan for ongoing observation: Plan how, when, and what you will observe during the first days and weeks of school (p. 37).

6 Consider how to involve children in the assessment process. Talk with them about how and why you observe them (p. 42).

7 Think about how you will use your observations in planning lessons and activities for each child (p. 44).

8 Decide how to report children's performance and progress to their families. Select the reporting option you will use (Chapter 5).

Collaborating with Colleagues

It is easier to begin a new initiative if you have the opportunity to talk it over and make plans with your colleagues. If several fellow teachers adopt this observation method along with you, it will be helpful to meet regularly in order to share concerns and solve problems that arise. You can learn a great deal from hearing how your colleagues have set up storage systems or documented observational information.

Teachers tell us that they have benefited greatly from regular informal conversations with colleagues as well as from professional development sessions scheduled every two to four weeks. These sessions can be used to:

- discuss progress and share strategies for resolving problems
- study sections of the Guidelines in order to develop a shared understanding of children's expected performance across the curriculum
- plan how to introduce Checklists to families
- share observation methods and management techniques
- develop reliability in making Checklist ratings
- decide upon a reporting method

Teachers' ongoing collaboration is extremely effective in supporting the process of implementation.

Chapter 2

Understanding the Work Sampling Developmental Guidelines and Checklists

THIS CHAPTER PRESENTS AND EXPLAINS THE WORK SAMPLING Developmental Guidelines and Checklists. It covers the following topics:

- Understanding Guidelines and Checklists

- Purposes of Guidelines and Checklists

- Organization and Structure of Guidelines and Checklists

Overview of the Guidelines and Checklists

What are they?

- **Developmental Guidelines** are a set of reasonable expectations used to evaluate student performance and achievement at different ages

- **Developmental Checklists** are lists of grade-specific performance indicators that are described in the Developmental Guidelines and are used for summarizing and interpreting your observations

What are their purposes?

1 To focus observation on particular knowledge, skills, and behavior
2 To summarize, record, and interpret observations
3 To provide a set of criteria for observation and evaluation based on national standards of curriculum and child development research
4 To help plan appropriate curriculum and instruction

What are their features?

- **Grade-Level Guidelines** contain the Guidelines for a single age/grade level and are designed for efficient classroom use with Checklists

- **Omnibus Guidelines** present Guidelines for six grade levels side-by-side to show continuous progress of performance indicators

- Checklists list performance indicators for a single grade level and provide space to rate students on each indicator three times per year

How do I use Guidelines and Checklists?

Before the school year begins:

- Gain familiarity with the Guidelines for your age/grade level
- Extend your knowledge and understanding of observation
- Investigate and prepare observation methods and tools
- Set up an organized storage system

During each reporting period:

- Plan, observe, and record
- Review Checklists periodically, making pencil ratings
- Talk with students about observation and expectations
- Apply what you learn to daily/weekly planning

Near the end of each reporting period:

- Review preliminary ratings
- Make final ratings
- Identify examples to share with families
- Select and implement a reporting method

Related Materials

- Reproducible Masters of Process Notes forms (see Appendix B)
- Wall Chart of Performance Indicators (included with Grade Level Guidelines)

Understanding Guidelines and Checklists

Children engage in many different classroom activities every day. They construct block buildings, participate in class meetings, solve problems using manipulatives, talk with their friends, and write in their journals. Systematic observation of students' behavior, actions, and language enables you, the teacher, to gather information about children's skills and knowledge. For example, a block structure may show a child's understanding of symmetry and sense of order. Comments during a class meeting may reveal a child's understanding of human similarities and differences. A child's solution to a math problem may demonstrate how she uses problem-solving strategies.

Using observational assessment effectively requires that you know what to look for, how to recognize features of children's learning at different ages, and the criteria for evaluating students fairly and reliably. The Work Sampling Developmental Guidelines outline developmentally appropriate expectations for students and help you focus your observations on significant skills, knowledge, and behaviors. They incorporate extensive research into national, state, and local standards and reflect widely-accepted expectations for children of different ages.

Effective observational assessment also requires an organizational tool that helps you manage your observations. The Developmental Checklist helps you organize what you have observed (the content of your observations) and your interpretations or evaluations. Without a Checklist, it is nearly impossible to focus on and remember the actions, behaviors, and language of 20 – 30 students for six to eight hours a day. The Checklist enables you to document and evaluate students' classroom activities by creating a detailed profile of each child's skills, knowledge, and behaviors.

Together, the Work Sampling Guidelines and Checklists provide a framework for observation, documentation, and evaluation. They can help you focus on students you do not yet know very well; remind you to observe all areas of your curriculum; assist you in determining when your instructional strategies are working and when they are not; and help you chart children's continuous progress in order to plan curriculum that reflects individual growth and change.

Purposes of Guidelines and Checklists

1 **To focus observation.** Guidelines and Checklists direct your attention to students' acquisition of particular knowledge, skills, and behaviors. The Guidelines and Checklists list and describe what you should look for at particular ages or grade levels.

2 **To summarize, record, and interpret observations.** Over a period of some months you will collect many observational records. Periodically, you review these records and give meaning to them, look for patterns, and assess what you know and do not know about each child. Every time you review and rate a student using the Checklist, you transfer a mass of observational data into a more manageable profile of the child's knowledge, skills, and behaviors.

3 **To provide valid criteria for evaluation.** The Guidelines describe reasonable expectations for children within a particular year so that teachers know what to expect of children at a given age or grade. These criteria, or standards, are based on information from national curriculum groups, state and local scope and sequences, and child development research. (A detailed list of all sources used in the development of the Guidelines is found in the Omnibus Guidelines volumes.) In addition, the Guidelines reflect the provisions of the National Education Goals Panel and the principles of Developmentally Appropriate Practices as defined by the National Association for the Education of Young Children. When you use these criteria, your evaluations of children will be more reliable and valid than when you use idiosyncratic, possibly inaccurate, ideas about what students should be able to do at different ages.

4 **To support curriculum and instruction.** Repeated review of the Guidelines is an excellent way to ensure that you are addressing all aspects of the curriculum in your classroom. Periodic review of children's Checklists ensures that some children are not being overlooked or missing out on important instructional opportunities. This type of ongoing monitoring of students' performance can remind you to use the information you acquire about children's skills and knowledge to plan and individualize instruction.

Organization and Structure of Guidelines and Checklists

The Work Sampling Guidelines and Checklists are based on seven categories or domains of classroom learning and curriculum. They identify and describe a set of developmentally appropriate skills, knowledge, and behaviors for children from three years old through fifth grade in each of seven domains.

DOMAIN A *domain* is defined as a broad area of a child's growth and learning. The following seven domains appear throughout all age/grade levels covered by the Work Sampling Guidelines and Checklists:

- Personal and Social Development
- Language and Literacy
- Mathematical Thinking
- Scientific Thinking
- Social Studies
- The Arts
- Physical Development & Health

Work Sampling Domains

Each domain is described below:

I Personal and Social Development. This domain emphasizes emotional and social competence. A teacher learns about children's emotional development — their sense of responsibility to themselves and others, how they feel about themselves and view themselves as learners — through ongoing observation, conversations with children, and information from family members. Teachers learn about children's social competence by interacting with them, observing their interactions with other adults and peers, and watching how they make decisions and solve social problems.

II Language and Literacy. This domain organizes the language and literacy skills needed to understand and convey meaning into five components: Listening, Speaking, Reading, Writing, and Research. Students acquire proficiency in this domain through extensive experience with language, print, and literature in a variety of contexts. Over time students learn to construct meaning, make connections to their own lives, and gradually begin to critically analyze and interpret what they hear, observe, and read. They begin to communicate effectively orally and in writing for different audiences and purposes.

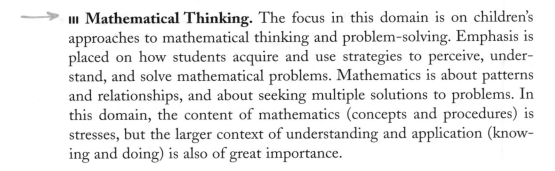

III Mathematical Thinking. The focus in this domain is on children's approaches to mathematical thinking and problem-solving. Emphasis is placed on how students acquire and use strategies to perceive, understand, and solve mathematical problems. Mathematics is about patterns and relationships, and about seeking multiple solutions to problems. In this domain, the content of mathematics (concepts and procedures) is stresses, but the larger context of understanding and application (knowing and doing) is also of great importance.

IV Scientific Thinking. This domain addresses central areas of scientific investigation: inquiry skills, physical, life, and earth sciences. The processes of scientific investigation are emphasized throughout because process skills are embedded in— and fundamental to— all science instruction and content. The domain's focus is on how children actively investigate through observing, recording, describing, questioning, forming explanations, and drawing conclusions.

V Social Studies. Encompassing history, economics, citizenship, and geography, the domain of social studies emphasizes social and cultural understanding. Children acquire this understanding from personal experiences and from the experiences of others. As children study present day and historical topics, they learn about human interdependence and the relationships between people and their environment. Throughout social studies, children use a variety of skills, including conducting research, using oral and visual sources, solving problems systematically, and making informed decisions using the democratic process.

VI The Arts. The emphasis in this domain is on children's engagement with the arts (dance, dramatics, music, and fine arts), both actively and receptively, rather than mastery of skills and techniques related to particular artistic media. The components address two ideas: how children use the arts to express, represent, and integrate their experiences, and how children develop an understanding and appreciation for the arts. It focuses on how opportunities to use and appreciate the arts enable children to demonstrate what they know, expand their thinking, and make connections among the arts, culture, history, and other domains.

VII Physical Development and Health. The emphasis in this domain is on physical development as an integral part of a child's well-being and educational growth. The components address gross motor skills, fine motor skills, and personal health and safety. A principal focus in gross motor is on children's ability to move in ways that demonstrate control, balance, and coordination. Fine motor skills are equally important in laying the groundwork for artistic expression, handwriting, and self-care skills. The third component addresses children's growing ability to understand and manage their personal health and safety.

FUNCTIONAL COMPONENT Each domain is divided into sub-sets or *functional components*. For example, the domain of Mathematical Thinking is composed of the following functional components:

- Mathematical processes
- Numbers and operations
- Patterns, relationships, and functions
- Geometry and spatial relations
- Measurement
- Data collection and probability (appears only in grades K–5)

Within each domain, most functional components appear throughout all eight age/grade levels of the Work Sampling Guidelines and Checklists. Some components, however, are appropriate only at particular grade levels. For example, in the domain of Mathematical Thinking, the component of data collection and probability appears only in grades K–5 because it is not developmentally appropriate for three and four year olds. In other cases, components are introduced in order to highlight their curricular importance at certain grade levels. At earlier age levels, the Omnibus Guidelines provide cross references to relevant indicators.

PERFORMANCE INDICATOR Finally, each functional component is composed of a set of *performance indicators*. Performance indicators present the skills, behaviors, attitudes, and accomplishments you will be teaching and assessing in the classroom. Performance indicators and the expectations described for them are specific to each grade level, changing gradually from grade to grade. Figure 1 shows the relationship among domain, functional components, and performance indicators for Language and Literacy. The performance indicators shown are from the first-grade Guidelines.

Grade Level Developmental Guidelines

Each of the Work Sampling eight grade level Developmental Guidelines (age 3 to grade 5) provides an overall view of what children can be expected to learn every year. Each performance indicator is elaborated with a *rationale* and several *examples*. The rationale explains the meaning of and justification for the performance indicator and briefly outlines reasonable expectations for children at a given age or grade.

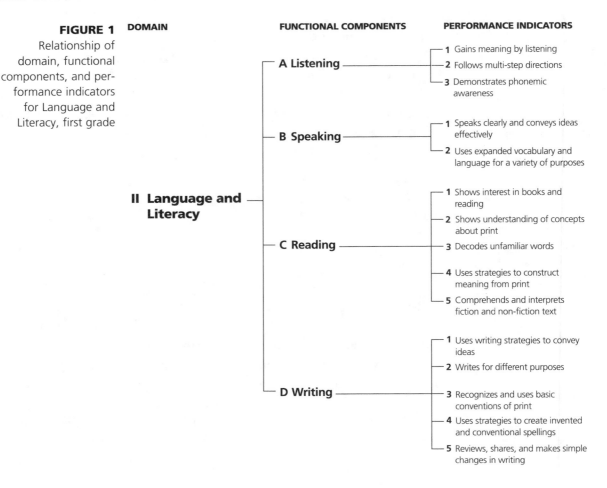

FIGURE 1

Relationship of
domain, functional
components, and per-
formance indicators
for Language and
Literacy, first grade

DOMAIN   FUNCTIONAL COMPONENTS   PERFORMANCE INDICATORS

**II Language and
Literacy**

A Listening

1 Gains meaning by listening

2 Follows multi-step directions

3 Demonstrates phonemic awareness

B Speaking

1 Speaks clearly and conveys ideas effectively

2 Uses expanded vocabulary and language for a variety of purposes

C Reading

1 Shows interest in books and reading

2 Shows understanding of concepts about print

3 Decodes unfamiliar words

4 Uses strategies to construct meaning from print

5 Comprehends and interprets fiction and non-fiction text

D Writing

1 Uses writing strategies to convey ideas

2 Writes for different purposes

3 Recognizes and uses basic conventions of print

4 Uses strategies to create invented and conventional spellings

5 Reviews, shares, and makes simple changes in writing

The three to five curriculum-embedded examples that follow each rationale show several ways children might demonstrate the skill, knowledge, or behavior within the context of the classroom. It is important to remember that these are only examples. Children have many ways of showing us what they know and can do. These examples are intended to remind us of this diversity and to serve as a catalyst for thinking about how individual children demonstrate their learning. You should not expect to see children perform all (or even any) of the examples given. Rather, the examples illustrate and give additional meaning to the performance indicators so that they can be interpreted similarly in different classrooms by different teachers.

The Developmental Guidelines are *criterion-referenced*. This means that a student's work is compared to specific criteria in each domain rather than to other students' work. During the development of the Guidelines, teachers, curriculum specialists, and administrators from around the country contributed extensively to shaping the content of the Guidelines.

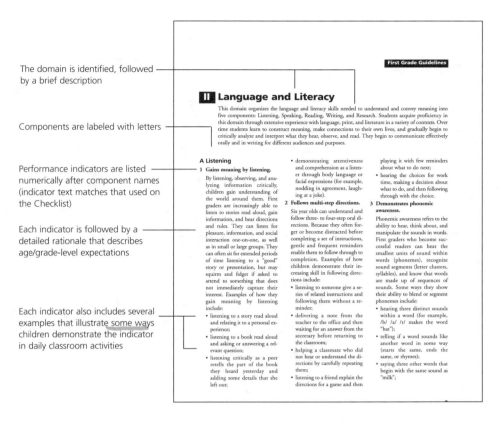

The domain is identified, followed by a brief description

Components are labeled with letters

Performance indicators are listed numerically after component names (indicator text matches that used on the Checklist)

Each indicator is followed by a detailed rationale that describes age/grade-level expectations

Each indicator also includes several examples that illustrate some ways children demonstrate the indicator in daily classroom activities

First Grade Guidelines

II Language and Literacy

This domain organizes the language and literacy skills needed to understand and convey meaning into five components: Listening, Speaking, Reading, Writing, and Research. Students acquire proficiency in this domain through extensive experience with language, print, and literature in a variety of contexts. Over time students learn to construct meaning, make connections to their own lives, and gradually begin to critically analyze and interpret what they hear, observe, and read. They begin to communicate effectively orally and in writing for different audiences and purposes.

A Listening

1 Gains meaning by listening.

By listening, observing, and analyzing information critically, children gain understanding of the world around them. First graders are increasingly able to listen to stories read aloud, gain information, and hear directions and rules. They can listen for pleasure, information, and social interaction one-on-one, as well as in small or large groups. They can often sit for extended periods of time listening to a "good" story or presentation, but may squirm and fidget if asked to attend to something that does not immediately capture their interest. Examples of how they gain meaning by listening include:

- listening to a story read aloud and relating it to a personal experience;
- listening to a book read aloud and asking or answering a relevant question;
- listening critically as a peer retells the part of the book they heard yesterday and adding some details that she left out;

- demonstrating attentiveness and comprehension as a listener through body language or facial expressions (for example, nodding in agreement, laughing at a joke).

2 Follows multi-step directions.

Six year olds can understand and follow three- to four-step oral directions. Because they often forget or become distracted before completing a set of instructions, gentle and frequent reminders enable them to follow through to completion. Examples of how children demonstrate their increasing skill in following directions include:

- listening to someone give a series of related instructions and following them without a reminder;
- delivering a note from the teacher to the office and then waiting for an answer from the secretary before returning to the classroom;
- helping a classmate who did not hear or understand the directions by carefully repeating them;
- listening to a friend explain the directions for a game and then

playing it with few reminders about what to do next;

- hearing the choices for work time, making a decision about what to do, and then following through with the choice.

3 Demonstrates phonemic awareness.

Phonemic awareness refers to the ability to hear, think about, and manipulate the sounds in words. First graders who become successful readers can hear the smallest units of sound within words (phonemes), recognize sound segments (letter clusters, syllables), and know that words are made up of sequences of sounds. Some ways they show their ability to blend or segment phonemes include:

- hearing three distinct sounds within a word (for example, /b/ /a/ /t/ makes the word "bat");
- telling if a word sounds like another word in some way (starts the same, ends the same, or rhymes);
- saying three other words that begin with the same sound as "milk";

Developmental Checklists

Developmental Checklists are double-page spreads showing all the domains, components, and performance indicators for a single age/grade level. Using a Checklist for each student, you review your observational data, make an interpretation, and then make evaluative ratings. This process is completed formally three times during the year (fall, winter, and spring). These three time periods are called *reporting periods*. You rate each indicator using the ratings "Not Yet," "In Process," or "Proficient." These ratings will be discussed more fully later in Chapter 3 (see page 41).

Along the right hand edge of the Checklist, there is space for identifying information about the child and the dates of the reporting period. Information on the back cover of the Checklist describes the Guidelines and Checklist and explains the ratings. This information is useful when a student transfers to a new school where teachers are unfamiliar with Work Sampling. The front cover of the Checklist includes space for you to record optional comments.

Understanding the Work Sampling
Developmental Guidelines and Checklists

Identifying information about the child is along the side

Domain names appear in black

Component names appear in black type on a colored bar
Indicators are listed for each component

Each indicator includes a page reference keyed to the grade level Guidelines

Each indicator includes space to make one of three ratings ("Not Yet," "In Process," "Proficient") during the fall, winter, and spring (F, W, S)

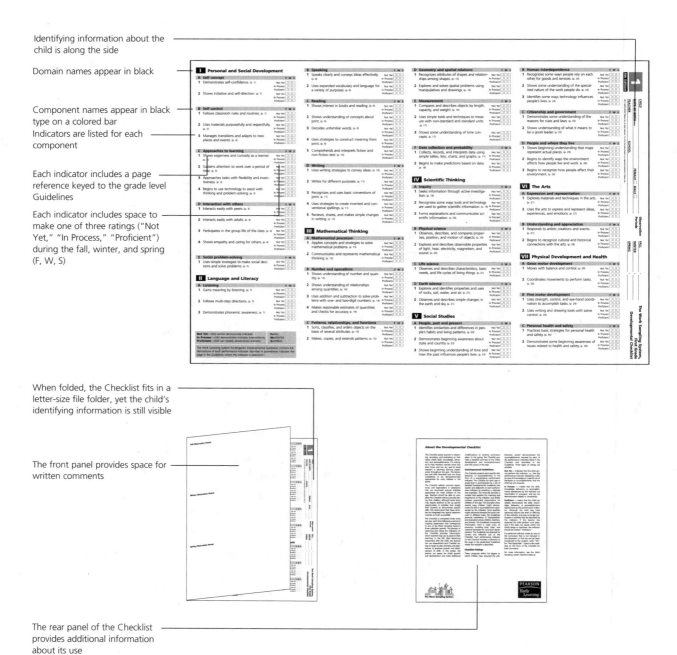

When folded, the Checklist fits in a letter-size file folder, yet the child's identifying information is still visible

The front panel provides space for written comments

The rear panel of the Checklist provides additional information about its use

Omnibus Guidelines

To illustrate and highlight the continuum of development, the Omnibus Guidelines combines six levels of the individual grade level Guidelines into a single volume. Each pair of facing pages shows the changes over time in a set of related performance indicators. Two volumes of the Omnibus Guidelines are available:

- Vol. 1: Preschool–Third Grade
- Vol. 2: Kindergarten–Fifth Grade

Many performance indicators appear consistently throughout all age/grade levels. However, in some cases performance indicators do not appear at each age/grade level. This may occur for one of four reasons.

- Sometimes a skill is not developmentally appropriate for a particular age/grade level. For example, in the domain of Mathematical Thinking and in the component probability and statistics, the first performance indicator at the kindergarten level is, "Begins to collect data and make records using lists or graphs." This skill is not an age-appropriate expectation for three year olds.

- Sometimes a performance indicator at one age/grade level appears in a slightly different order within the domain than the same or similar performance indicator at a different age/grade level. For example, in the domain of Language and Literacy and in the component of reading, the performance indicator "Decodes unfamiliar words" appears as the third indicator for first grade. However, the same indicator appears as the second indicator for second grade.

- In some cases a skill is not assessed at a particular age/grade level because the skill is not yet age-appropriate. However, children may have begun to work on the skill. For example, in the domain of Language and Literacy and the component of spelling, there is no kindergarten performance indicator comparable to the first grade indicator, "Uses strategies to create invented and conventional spellings." In kindergarten the age-appropriate, related indicator is "Uses letter-like shapes, symbols, letters, and words to convey meaning."

- Sometimes a performance indicator does not appear at an age/grade level because it is no longer a curricular focus and is embedded in another indicator. For example, in the domain of Mathematical

Thinking, and the component of patterns, relationships, and functions, the first performance indicator at the second grade level is "Sorts, classifies, and compares objects using attributes and quantities." This performance indicator does not appear at the third, fourth, and fifth grade levels.

Each domain appears in the Omnibus Guidelines in its own section and begins with a brief description

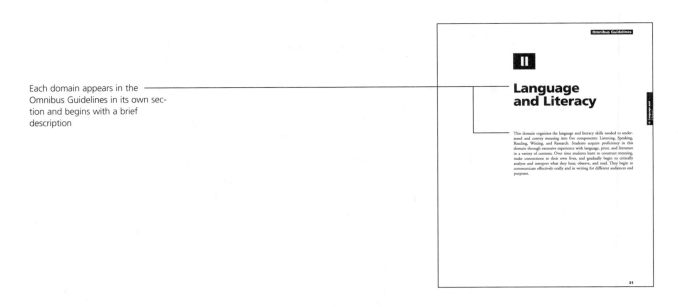

Each pair of facing pages displays the performance indicators from six age or grade levels

Functional component

Each indicator is followed by the same rationale and examples that appear in the grade-level Guidelines

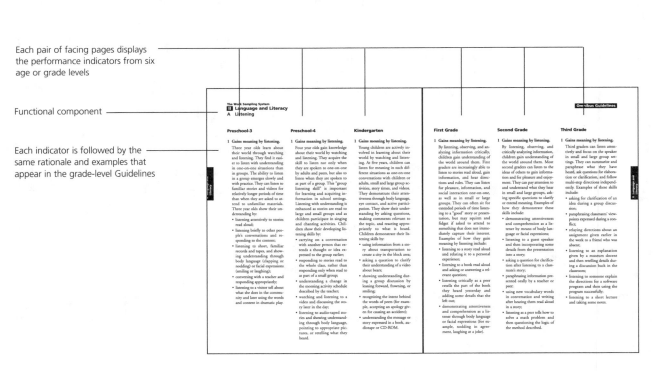

Chapter 3

How to Use Guidelines and Checklists

USING GUIDELINES AND CHECKLISTS INVOLVES DIFFERENT TASKS AT different times of the school year, all directed toward making observation and recording an integral part of your classroom life.

Guidelines and Checklist Timeline

The timeline depicts the schedule for activities associated with the Guidelines and Checklist for a single reporting period.

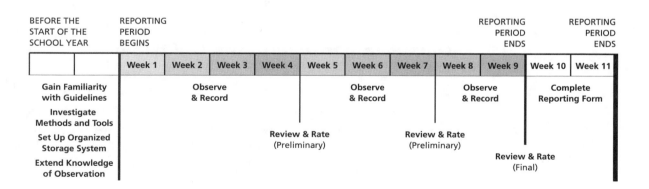

- **Before** the school year begins, four preparatory steps will require your time and attention: 1) becoming familiar with the Guidelines, 2) learning about the process of observation, 3) setting up organizational systems, and 4) establishing observational methods.

- **During** each reporting period, you maintain routines of observing and recording, periodically reviewing students' Checklists so that your observations stay focused and your curriculum is responsive to each student.

- **Near the end** of each reporting period, you turn your attention to summarizing your knowledge about students and identifying examples for reporting to families.

Before the School Year Begins

Before the children arrive in the fall we recommend that you begin the following activities. These tasks are significant when you are learning to use the Work Sampling Guidelines and Checklists, but will require less time after the first year of implementation.

- Gain familiarity with the Guidelines.
- Extend your knowledge and understanding of observation.
- Investigate and prepare observation methods and tools.
- Set up an organized storage system.

Gain Familiarity with the Guidelines

Familiarizing yourself with the Guidelines for your age/grade level is the first step to integrating this observational assessment into your life as a teacher. Once familiar with the Guidelines, you can plan curriculum and instruction with confidence that you have the information needed to assess your students. Many teachers report that their understanding of the Guidelines helps them to be more focused in their curriculum planning. As you assess students using observation, knowing the Guidelines will make it easier to decide what to look for and pay attention to. You develop clearer expectations for students, leading to greater consistency in your observations and judgments about children. There are many ways to become more familiar with the Guidelines. We suggest these four:

- Read one domain at a time
- Discuss the Guidelines with colleagues
- Add your own examples
- Use the Wall Chart

READ ONE DOMAIN AT A TIME Reading and studying the Guidelines repeatedly is the primary way to become familiar with them. One or two complete readings can be followed by focusing on one domain at a time until you feel comfortable with the content. Teachers have invented many unique ways of keeping the Guidelines in the forefront of their minds. A common approach is to read them as you do weekly curriculum planning.

DISCUSS THE GUIDELINES WITH COLLEAGUES Discussing the Guidelines with colleagues offers many benefits. Conversation about the Guidelines leads to a shared understanding of the contents of each domain. Teachers of different grade levels gain an appreciation for the subtle developmental changes that occur as children grow. Moreover, you will better recognize and appreciate commonalities among curricula at different age/grade levels. A fifth grade teacher, for example, may come to recognize that early experiences with math manipulatives lay the groundwork for more sophisticated understanding of numerical concepts and operations.

Groups of teachers often study each domain together and compare their own local or state curriculum guides with the Work Sampling Guidelines. Another benefit of discussing the Guidelines with colleagues is that the group will develop a more consistent understanding of expectations for children; Checklist ratings from teacher to teacher will become more consistent and reliable. These collegial conversations are crucial when an entire school or system is working to implement the Guidelines and Checklists.

ADD YOUR OWN EXAMPLES Adding examples of your own to those listed in the Guidelines will help you internalize the performance indicators and rationales and make them more useful in your classroom. Remember that the examples listed are not comprehensive. They show only some of the ways that children demonstrate their knowledge and skills. One way that teachers have personalized the Work Sampling Guidelines is by adding examples that reflect the cultural backgrounds of their students. We encourage you to add examples from your students that show how they demonstrate their knowledge and skills.

USE THE WALL CHART Using the **WALL CHART OF PERFORMANCE INDICATORS** that accompanies each set of grade-level Guidelines is a convenient way to keep the domains, functional components, and performance indicators in your frame of reference. Post it in a place where you, students, and families can see and refer to it easily. It is a way of saying, "This is what is important to learn in this classroom. These are the things I teach, and these are the things I expect children to learn."

Extend Your Knowledge and Understanding of Observation

Before the school year begins, teachers new to Work Sampling can prepare themselves to use the Guidelines and Checklists by becoming knowledgeable about the processes of observation and recording. These processes are essential to using the Guidelines and Checklists successfully. Observation provides the evidence that you will use to support your evaluations of students.

In this section, we will discuss five key ideas:

- Definition of observation
- What you can learn from observing children
- Why classroom-based and ongoing observation is important
- Reasons for recording observation
- Differentiating between fact and interpretation

DEFINITION OF OBSERVATION Observation is defined as watching or regarding with attention or purpose in order to see or learn something. Observation allows us to learn about children by carefully watching them, listening to them, and studying their work. The following are some ways that you can observe students to learn more about them:

- ask questions that encourage them to describe their thinking

- listen to them as they describe how they made decisions and solved problems

- watch them as they play and work with materials and other children

- hold conferences with them about their work

- listen as they talk with others informally and during group discussions

- study their work (e.g., projects, writing, drawings, reports, learning logs, journals)

WHAT YOU CAN LEARN FROM OBSERVING CHILDREN Children tell us a great deal about who they are, what they know, and how they think by their actions and language. Careful observation over time can reveal important information about children's individual strengths and difficulties. It can also reveal not only what children know but how they came to know it—their process of thinking and learning. Observation helps you answer myriad questions you have about each student:

- How does this child approach tasks?

- How does this child use language to express thinking?

- What is this child's typical method of expression (e.g., drama, drawing, verbal language, body language)?

- How does this child use materials?

- How does this child engage in social tasks with others?

The answers to these questions are most readily obtained from classroom-based observation.

WHY CLASSROOM-BASED AND ONGOING OBSERVATION IS IMPORTANT Observational assessment gives a representative and complete view of a child. Because classroom observation occurs in a context that is familiar and comfortable for the child, you are likely to acquire an accurate picture of this child as a learner. Children's behavior is not influenced by "test anxiety" or misinterpreted because the child does not understand the directions to a task, as can happen with other types of assessment. The information you collect from observation reveals not only whether or not the child solved a problem correctly, but also illustrates the manner in which the child approached the task and solved the problem.

Moreover, observation is a valid way to assess children. It provides you with repeated opportunities to witness children practicing skills, demonstrating knowledge, and exhibiting behaviors in real—not simulated—learning activities. For example, one day you might photograph the castle a preschool student constructed in the block area. On another day, you might draw a quick sketch of the pattern block design she made in the math center. On yet a third occasion, you might save the collage she made by gluing shapes into a design. When you are ready to evaluate her performance and progress, your judgments about her sense of balance and symmetry will be based on these and many other observations rather than on a single example of her work.

REASONS FOR RECORDING OBSERVATIONS Recording your observations of children is important for at least four reasons. First, records help you remember and keep track of what children know and can do. Second, your documented observations provide the evidence to support your evaluations of children. Third, observations recorded over time enable you to see patterns in children's behaviors and their approach to learning. These patterns are often evident to us only when we reflect on collections of observational notes. Finally, records of observations will help you plan instructional activities that are responsive to children's interests, strengths, and needs.

DIFFERENTIATING BETWEEN FACT AND INTERPRETATION Documenting observations effectively requires that you differentiate between what you actually see and hear, and your own opinions and interpretations of these actions. Language that describes the actions of children at work and play is more informative than words that convey judgment. For example, Jeremy, a first grader, is working with Cuisenaire rods to solve a series of math problems. Examples 1 and 2 show how two teachers might document his work.

EXAMPLE 1   11/4 10 a.m.—Jeremy is scattered and too distracted to do his work.

EXAMPLE 2   11/4 10 a.m.—Jeremy has worked on math for 15 min—completed one problem of five. Builds with rods. Talks continually w/others about baseball. Walked to and from pencil sharpener and water fountain many times.

Although both records convey that Jeremy is not completing his math work, the first gives only the teacher's impressions. The second record describes Jeremy's actions and provides enough detailed information to explain why he is not completing his work. It allows you to ask questions about how to support Jeremy's success as a learner: Is Jeremy distracted? Is his interest in baseball absorbing his attention? Would it help to engage Jeremy's interest by relating the math problems to baseball? Would he be more successful if he could work collaboratively on the problems with others? Questions and interpretations/impressions can be included in the documentation of an observation, but should be clearly identified as such. As shown in Example 3, some teachers divide their records into two parts. On one side they write observations. On the other side they note questions, concerns, and interpretations of behavior.

EXAMPLE 3	Notes	Interpretations
	11/4: 10 a.m. Jeremy has worked on math for 15 min—completed one problem of five. Builds with rods. Talks continually w/others about baseball. Walked to and from pencil sharpener and water fountain many times.	Distracted? Why?

be objective

Investigate and Prepare Observation Methods and Tools

Although you have experience informally observing your students, observing systematically and recording your observations may be less familiar to you. Before you begin to observe and record we encourage you to consider three issues:

• The context for observation
• How to record observational information
• Tools for recording observations

The Context for Observation

Teachers observe and record children's learning in three different situations:

• Participating in the action
• Stepping out of the action
• Reflecting on the action after the fact

PARTICIPATING IN THE ACTION As a teacher, you are typically in the midst of classroom action. You might be conferring with a single student, guiding a small group through a lesson, or having a discussion with the entire class. At the same time, you are watching children, listening to them, taking mental notes about who is working with whom, and asking questions that extend children's thinking. Clearly, you are gathering a wealth of information as you interact in the classroom. Perhaps the biggest challenge of using the Work Sampling Guidelines and Checklists is finding effective, efficient methods to create a written record of important information so that you do not have to rely solely on memory. A thorough discussion of the options available for recording your observations begins on page 26.

It is essential to establish realistic expectations about how much is possible to record as you observe in the action. You should not expect to record every behavior or word. The records you make may seem brief and lacking in detail compared to the records you make when you step out of the action or reflect on students' learning at a later time. When you are working or talking with one child, you may be able to record sentence-length comments and anecdotal notes. But when you are leading a class discussion or working with a group of children, you have to limit your recording to shorthand notes or checkmarks and other symbols that have meaning to you.

Figure 2 shows how a third grade teacher documented her observations when observing during the action. This teacher was leading a class discussion about a conflict that occurred on the playground. During the discussion she noted the students who participated and when relevant, she added a quick comment describing their participation.

Figure 2
Teacher-created matrix allows the teacher to monitor children's participation during class discussions

Class Meeting Observations   Date: _4/12/99_

Topic: _Discuss playground conflict/soccer_

NOTE: P   -participated somewhat
Nick and Victor had argument   PA -participated actively
Nick requested the meeting   Q   -quiet

Names		Comments and Reflections
Alex	PA	V and N argued last year
Bonita	P	"this happens w/ other kids too" suggested 2 play areas
Carla	Q	
Collin	P	
Devan	PA	related personal stories
Ekker	P	sug. N & V write apology ltrs.
Frank	PA	asked N & V qstns for details
Horace	abs	
Ingrid	Q	
Kate	PA	volunteered as note taker
Lara	P	"Nick, maybe you and Victor should play in different games"
Marcus	PA	
Nick	PA	told conflict clearly - owned responsibility
Paul	Q	seemed focused -
Rajit	P	
Roxanne	PA	begins all w/ well, I think... many comments not related
Shayna	P	
Trina	abs	
Victor	P	hesitant to speak much - shrugs w/ ideas, I'll try it...to L's idea

Whether you are working with a single child or a group, planning and focusing are important keys to successful observational recording. Thinking ahead of time about the purpose of an activity and what you expect to observe will help you devise recording methods and tools that will facilitate the observation process.

STEPPING OUT OF THE ACTION Stepping out of the action to observe is an extremely effective way to learn about children. It allows you to focus on one child at a time. You may watch how the child interacts with others or how the child approaches a learning task. When you are in the midst of classroom action, you do many things simultaneously—motivating children, communicating information, keeping children engaged, providing materials, and teaching skills. By stepping out of the action, however, you can suspend these tasks for a few moments and be completely observant of the activities around you.

Stepping out of the action to observe does not require large amounts of time. Take three to five minutes to step back and observe one or two children. You will be surprised by how much data you can collect in a short time. Rather than being overly ambitious and setting aside large amounts of time, it is more effective to develop the habit of observing out of the action for just a few minutes three or four times each week. Example 4 shows anecdotal notes taken by a preschool teacher while stepping out of the action:

EXAMPLE 4

4/6 Recci: Dramatic Play
As I approach the house area, Recci is playing with the doctor's kit. He silently administers oxygen to a doll, takes its temperature, and tests its reflexes. He uses the stethoscope and says, "I can hear his heart for real." He uses the blood pressure cuff, asking for help from Lisa in attaching it to the doll's arm.

Iola enters the house area, and asks Lisa who is also playing in the house, "Who are you being?" She replies, "Doctor." Iola then asks Recci. He says, "A nurse." Iola asks, "What can I be?" Recci says, "You're the mom." He hands her the doll and gives the doll a shot. He says, "Ouch!"

REFLECTING ON THE ACTION AFTER THE FACT Reflecting after the fact suggests two different types of teacher actions. The first involves taking a moment after an event occurs or at the end of the day to document what transpired. The second entails reviewing children's work as a way to reflect on their learning.

You probably make mental notes in the midst of classroom action all the time. By taking a few minutes during a break in the day (for example, during rest time, quiet reading, or journal time) or at the end of a day you can record some notes about events that occurred. Recall a math period and some of the strategies children used, or a discussion and some comments children made. It is both unnecessary and unrealistic to think about recording something about every child or every event in the day. However, when you get in the habit of making a few notes about one or two children or events each day or every few days, these records add up to a substantial written record of what children know and can do.

When you review children's work at the end of the day or week, the notes you make about children's learning inform the Checklist. What does the work show? What skills and knowledge are expressed in the work? Does the work reflect the assignment? Looking at children's work will also remind you of the context in which the work was created. What was the child doing? What was the activity? How did the child approach the task? Did the child show interest in the task? What else was going on in the classroom at that time? By jotting down these reflections you will have valuable information to help you complete the Checklist. These notes will also come in handy when you are trying to complete reports for parents or are preparing for conferences. Reviewing a domain of the Guidelines or Checklist prior to looking at children's work can help to focus your reflection. Example 5 illustrates a preschool teacher's reflection after the fact.

EXAMPLE 5   Nkrumah is currently working on controlling the mouse on the computer. He understands that he needs to put the cursor arrow on an object to activate it, but has difficulty coordinating movements to do so. When using the keyboard, he presses the screen occasionally instead of pressing a key.

How to Record Observational Information

RECORDING METHODS Teachers find many ways to record observational data in the classroom. Each technique makes different demands on a teacher's time and energy, and each provides a different type of information. Most teachers find that they use multiple methods. Deciding upon methods to use depends on the type of information you are trying to capture and the amount of observation time you have during classroom activities.

For example, if you are interested in how a child thinks, solves problems, uses materials, and interacts with others, select a method that allows for some descriptive writing. On the other hand, if you simply want to know whether a child is speaking during class meetings or the materials a child chooses during math time or the colors a child names accurately, select a method that involves checking or tallying.

When you are working with one child, in a reading or writing conference for example, you are able to take notes that describe what the child is doing quite clearly. However, when you are circulating around the classroom guiding children's involvement in a science project, making quick checkmarks on a matrix is easier to manage.

Selecting a documentation method depends on several factors: what you want to learn, the activities children are engaged in, and your responsibilities at the time of observation. Descriptions and samples of several different recording methods follow.

• **Brief notes** are quick written records that serve as a reminder of observed events. In Example 6, the teacher jotted a brief note that described how R.L., a third grader, showed his understanding of a story through his participation in his reading group.

EXAMPLE 6

1/15 R.L.
skit of Mrs. BEF w/TW, GK, ES
org. grp into roles
R acted w/express—phys + verb
repeated reminders to grp that seq. of skit follow story

• **Anecdotal notes** are more detailed narrative accounts that describe a particular event factually. Often they are created by jotting down brief notes and adding details later. They provide rich, detailed information. Example 7 is an anecdotal record from a preschool teacher who stepped out of the action to observe Dwight's participation in a cooking activity.

EXAMPLE 7

11/5 Dwight
Dwight is at the table cooking cranberries with Brian and Nancy (assistant). He is seated on his chair leaning over the table with his elbows on his chin. His lips are pursed and he is frowning a little bit. He watches. B stirs with the wooden spoon. D says, "I see smoke." Suger, water, and cranberries are heating on the hot plate. N says, "This is steam, Dwight. Not smoke." D says, giggling, "Brian, that steam's getting on your face." He sits up on his knees, his two hands on the table. "I want to stir now. I want steam in my face." He takes the spoon and begins to stir, putting his face near the pot.

• **Running records** are detailed narrative accounts of behavior recorded in a sequential manner, just as it happens. They include all behavior that occurs within a given time frame. Like anecdotal notes, they provide rich information, but require you to step out of the action.

EXAMPLE 8

Nikki and Josepha are standing side-by-side at the water table, Josepha is pouring water from a cup measure into a small-mouthed bottle. Much of the water spills into the water table instead of going into the bottle. Nikki gives Josepha a funnel saying, "Use this so the water won't leak out of the bottle." Josepha takes it and puts it onto the top of the bottle; it's too big to fit down into the bottle. She wraps her right fist around the seam between the funnel and the bottle and continues to pour with her left hand. Nikki watches. After four more cupfuls, he crouches down and looks on the shelf under the table. He finds a bottle with a wider mouth and brings it up, saying to Josepha, "The funnel will definitely fit in this one and then you can use both of your hands."

Interpretation: Nikki—expressive language, problem solving

Josepha—works silently, exploring

• **Rating scales** are tools that indicate the degree to which a student possesses a certain skill (Figure 3).

Figure 3

Simple check marks are sufficient to record detailed information using rating scales

Child: _Tony_   Date: _2/16/00_   Time: _2:00 PM_

Observer: _Mrs. R._

Behavior	Rating			
	Always	Usually	Never	N/A
Makes contribution to discussion		✓		
Contributions relevant to topic			✓	
Looks at person speaking	✓			
Asks questions of other contributors	✓			

• **Matrices** provide a way to write very brief notes or make a simple rating of a skill or set of skills for a few children or for the entire class. Names of students are listed on the left-hand side of a page. Specific skills, concepts, or behaviors are listed across the top. Figure 4 illustrates a matrix created by a kindergarten teacher for use during small group activities. She fills in children's names and the skills she plans to observe during the activity. In this example she added some notes below the matrix.

Figure 4
The teacher created this matrix to be used for observations during group activities

Math Activity: _Spin a Step_   **Date:** _12/18/99_

I -Independently
H -with help
N -no

Names	Shows interest in the game	Follows rules	Plays cooperatively	Maintains focus	Counts accurately	Adds to solve problem
Ben	I	H	H*	I	I	I
Elise	H	I	I	H	I	H*
George	N	H	H	N*	H	H
Patsy	I	I	I	I	H*	N*

Notes:

Ben didn't want to give up the spinner when it was the next person's turn
Held it, kept spinning it, put it on the floor

Elise read the numbers on spinner, moved correct # of spaces, needed cubes to do addition

George wandered off between turns; said I hate this game when the spinner landed on a number he couldn't use

Patsy needs practice with numbers to be successful w/game. Others gave her help

• **Tallies** are used to count the instances of a particular behavior or event during a predetermined time interval. Figure 5 shows an example of how a kindergarten teacher used a tally to record children's choices during the course of a week. Each week she monitored the activities of five children during "free choice time." Each day of the week she noted the choice the child made at the beginning of the period. If they moved to another choice, she noted it with an additional mark in a different column. The information she gathered from this documentation method helped her learn about children's interests and their willingness to select different activities within the classroom. She used this information to make instructional decisions that build on and extend children's interests.

Figure 5
A tally provides an efficient method for recording children's choices

Choice Record
Week of: _4/8–12_

Names	Blocks	Table Toys	Art	Computer	Dram. Play	Writing Ctr	Library
Annie	I			II	III		
Brian		P I	PPP III				II
Maya	II		C I	I		II	I
Shayguan			DCC III	I	II		
Tyrell	III	LL II		II			

L - Lego   D - Draw
M - Math manip   p - Paint
P - Puzzles   C - Collage

• **Time samplings** are used to record the frequency of a behavior over time. Time samplings can be helpful when you need very specific information about a particular aspect of a child's behavior. Figure 6 illustrates how a teacher used a time sampling to monitor a student's ability to sustain attention on a task. She will use the information she gains from this documentation method to help establish a behavior plan for the child.

Figure 6
A time sampling helps teachers monitor a student's abilities

Time Sample

Child: _Samantha_   Date: _3/12_   Time: _2:00 PM_

Activity: _Group Project Work_

1:00	1:05	1:10	1:15	1:20	1:25	1:30
OT	I	OT	OT	I	I	I

I – Involved (focused on activity, working with others on the task, contributing to the group's work)
OT – Off task (wandering around the room, engaging with others unrelated to the task, sitting alone and not working)

• **Diagrams, sketches, and photographs** capture the details of certain types of activities and projects, yet do not require lengthy writing. Older students can create these types of records themselves. In Figure 7, Ms. Q. sketched Oliver's response to the house building task.

Figure 7
The diagram in this example captures detail without lengthy writing

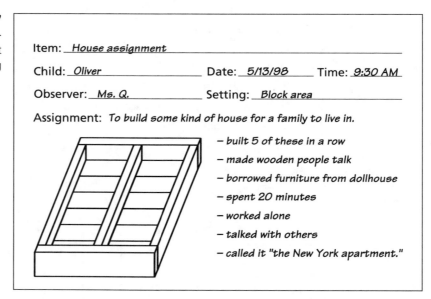

Item: _House assignment_

Child: _Oliver_   Date: _5/13/98_   Time: _9:30 AM_

Observer: _Ms. Q._   Setting: _Block area_

Assignment: _To build some kind of house for a family to live in._

– built 5 of these in a row
– made wooden people talk
– borrowed furniture from dollhouse
– spent 20 minutes
– worked alone
– talked with others
– called it "the New York apartment."

• **Audiotapes and videotapes** are excellent ways to capture children's language. Skits, puppet shows, story telling, and reading aloud lend themselves to this method of documentation.

TOOLS FOR RECORDING OBSERVATIONS Depending on the recording methods you choose, you will need a variety of tools to carry out your observations efficiently and effectively. The possibilities range from simple materials like note pads and index cards to sophisticated electronic devices. It is critical to think ahead and prepare what you are apt to need so your tools are ready once you begin observing. Consider the following possibilities:

• **Mailing labels** Attach a strip or sheet of labels to a clipboard. After jotting notes on a label, remove it and put it in the child's Teacher File. These labels can also be pre-printed and dated using a computer. (Teacher Files are described beginning on page 36.)

• **Legal pads** Use large pads to accommodate a whole class list or place smaller ones in several key locations around the classroom so there is always one nearby. Attach a pen or pencil to the pad. Figure 8 shows how one teacher modified a legal pad to fit her observation needs.

Figure 8
A teacher-created method for recording observations over time. The left margins of all pages but the last are cut away. The class list is written on the last page. Each day, a new page is used to record observations.

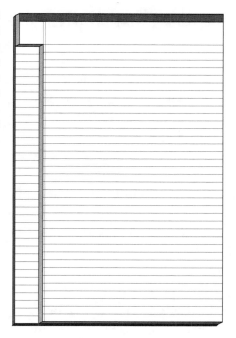

• **Index cards** Attach a card for each child to a file folder with tape so that the cards overlap. Alternatively, color-code them by domain and store on a ring or file them in a box.

• **Calendars** Some teachers keep a calendar for each month for each child on a ring or in a notebook. They keep daily notes on as many children as possible and then, at the end of a month, file the calendar in each child's

Teacher File. Weekly calendars and large desk calendars have also been used for recording observations.

• **Butcher paper** Hang butcher paper around the room and make notes directly on the paper or attach self-stick removeable notes to it.

• **Masking tape** Make notes on the tape, tear pieces off, and file in the child's Teacher File.

• **Self-stick removable notes** These come in a variety of colors and sizes and can be used on calendars, Work Sampling Process Note forms, or placed directly in students' Teacher Files.

• **Carpenters' aprons** Wearing a carpenter's apron enables some teachers to have removeable notes and pens ready to record spontaneous as well as planned observational notes.

• **Tape recorders** Use a tape recorder to dictate your observations. The disadvantage of this tool is that the taped information must be transcribed.

• **Still cameras** Many teachers find taking a photograph a quick way to capture a record of an event or product. You can solicit your school's parent organization, media center, or your classroom's parents to help pay for film and processing. Some teachers ask for rolls of film as part of the required school supplies at the beginning of the school year.

• **Video cameras** These are useful tools for documenting active work.

• **Hand-held computers** More teachers are using Palm Pilots to input observational data. These systems generally allow data to be sorted by student, date, and domain.

WORK SAMPLING PROCESS NOTE FORMS Work Sampling provides several forms designed to facilitate the recording process. Use of these forms is entirely optional. They are provided in Appendix B and can be reproduced or adapted to meet your specific needs.

The **DOMAIN PROCESS NOTES** form (Figure 9) has three columns and shows all seven domains. You can use this form to record observations for all developmental domains either for three children or for one child at three different times.

Figure 9
Domain Process Notes Form

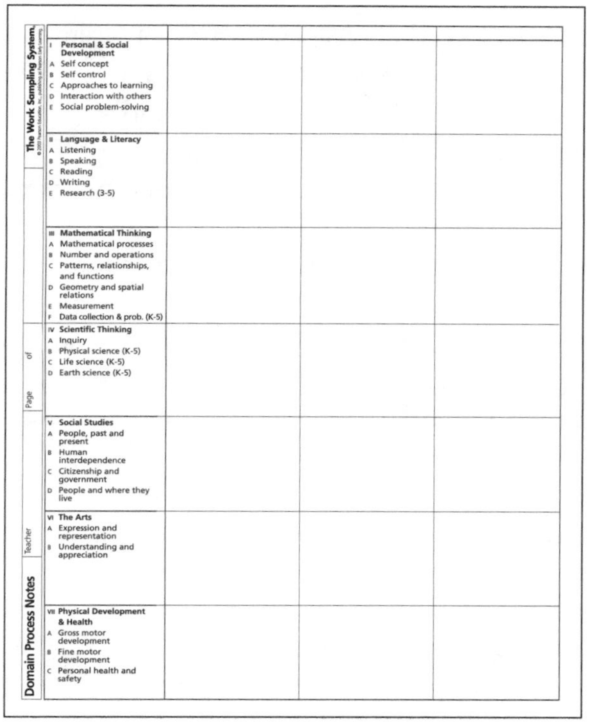

Domain Process Notes
The Work Sampling System.
Teacher
Page of

I Personal & Social Development
A Self concept
B Self control
C Approaches to learning
D Interaction with others
E Social problem-solving

II Language & Literacy
A Listening
B Speaking
C Reading
D Writing
E Research (3-5)

III Mathematical Thinking
A Mathematical processes
B Number and operations
C Patterns, relationships, and functions
D Geometry and spatial relations
E Measurement
F Data collection & prob. (K-5)

IV Scientific Thinking
A Inquiry
B Physical science (K-5)
C Life science (K-5)
D Earth science (K-5)

V Social Studies
A People, past and present
B Human interdependence
C Citizenship and government
D People and where they live

VI The Arts
A Expression and representation
B Understanding and appreciation

VII Physical Development & Health
A Gross motor development
B Fine motor development
C Personal health and safety

The **Child Domain Process Notes** form (Figure 10) is divided into eight boxes of equal size, one for each domain and one for additional comments. It is designed to document observations for all seven domains for one child.

Figure 10
Child Domain Process Notes form

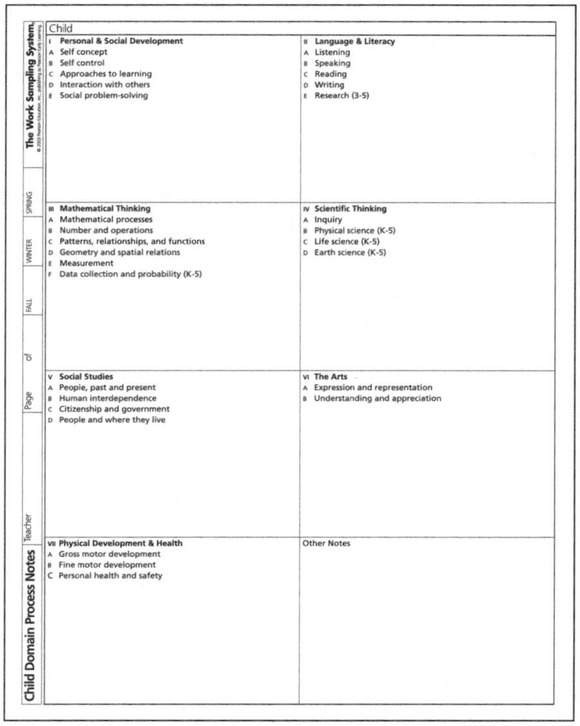

Child Domain Process Notes
The Work Sampling System.
Teacher
Page of
FALL WINTER SPRING
Child

I Personal & Social Development
A Self concept
B Self control
C Approaches to learning
D Interaction with others
E Social problem-solving

II Language & Literacy
A Listening
B Speaking
C Reading
D Writing
E Research (3-5)

III Mathematical Thinking
A Mathematical processes
B Number and operations
C Patterns, relationships, and functions
D Geometry and spatial relations
E Measurement
F Data collection and probability (K-5)

IV Scientific Thinking
A Inquiry
B Physical science (K-5)
C Life science (K-5)
D Earth science (K-5)

V Social Studies
A People, past and present
B Human interdependence
C Citizenship and government
D People and where they live

VI The Arts
A Expression and representation
B Understanding and appreciation

VII Physical Development & Health
A Gross motor development
B Fine motor development
C Personal health and safety

Other Notes

The GENERAL PROCESS NOTES form (Figure 11) consists of a 20-box grid with space to write children's names or dates of observations at the top of each box. It is open-ended and can be used in many ways, for example, to observe 20 children once, or five children at four different times, or four children during the course of a week. The boxes are the size of a small self-stick removeable note (1-½" x 2"). Using these notes will enable you to transfer them to a child's folder easily and effectively. Some teachers write directly on the forms; after the forms are completed they are cut up and placed in children's observation folders.

Figure 11
General Process Notes
form

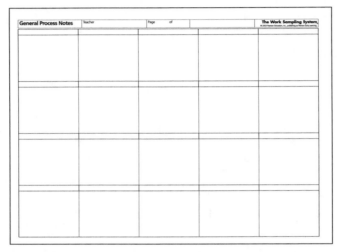

The ROSTER PROCESS NOTES form (Figure 12) provides a basic matrix for recording brief notes, coded entries, or other information for up to 30 children on one sheet.

Figure 12
Roster Process Notes form

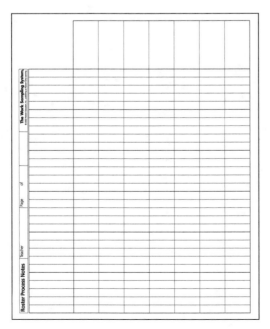

USING WORK SAMPLING PROCESS NOTES The figures that follow illustrate several ways that teachers have used the Work Sampling Process Notes. Figure 13 shows how a second grade teacher used the Domain Process Notes form to record her observations on two children. She used the same form for one week.

Figure 13

Part of a second grade teacher's completed Domain Process Notes form

Week of 2/14	Juanita	Whitney	
II Language & Literacy A Listening B Speaking C Reading D Writing E Research (3-5)	2/15 worked w/B.G. & R.T. on book skit; came to me 4x for help dealing with B & R	2/16 org. puppet show during choice stayed w/it for 45 min. presented it to the class	
III Mathematical Thinking A Mathematical processes B Number and operations C Patterns, relationships, and functions D Geometry and spatial relations E Measurement F Data collection & prob. (K-5)	2/14 wrote long story in journal — wnated to count total p. said "I can count the p. and times it by 2 to get all my sides." 2/16	2/15 3 color pattern AABCAABC w/unifix 2/16 reversals w/numbers 2/15	
IV Scientific Thinking A Inquiry B Physical science (K-5) C Life science (K-5) D Earth science (K-5) **V Social Studies**	Observed guinea pig w/ Nikki - spent timemaking detailed record of how g.p. eats	commented on layering of snow & ice in playgrd. Predicted it would take longer to melt than reg. snow because it was "packed so tight"	

The Work Sampling System™ © 2003 Pearson Education, Inc., publishing as Pearson Early Learning.

Figure 14 shows how a third grade teacher used the Child Domain Process Notes form to document observations about one child during a two-week period.

Figure 14

Part of a third grade teacher's completed Child Domain Process Notes form

I Personal & Social Development A Self concept B Self control C Approaches to learning D Interaction with others E Social problem-solving 3/9 In a fight w/Rodney about rules for soccer— came in from recess sweating and frowning— stomped around, would not sit down to talk	II Language & Literacy A Listening B Speaking C Reading D Writing E Research (3-5) 3/7 conf. w/him about story, he revised the ending to make it clear. He identified some spelling errors 3/18 conf. interested in Nolan Ryan-checked out book about Famous Pitchers said he knew N.R. would be in it. read 2 ch. for contract
III Mathematical Thinking A Mathematical processes B Number and operations	IV Scientific Thinking A Inquiry B Physical science (K-5)

Figure 15 shows how the same third grade teacher recorded observations about her students' writing.

Figure 15

Part of a third grade teacher's completed General Process Notes form

General Process Notes	Teacher	Page of	
Nikki	Jennifer	Albert	
3/11 Conf. to brain-storm gymnastics story. Shared her Xmas story. Good character development. Humorous "Book language" used to make transitions	3/7 Shared "The Cat, the Dog, the Bird, and Their Incredible Adventure." Works well from brainstorm. Learning to use quotation marks.	3/8 Conferenced with him about Jill or Owen story. He made revisions to make ending more clear. Also identified some spelling errors (3/7 computer)	

Figure 16 shows how a teacher monitored children's skills in recounting events in their writing. After deciding on certain skills to teach during writers' workshop for a week, the teacher set up the Roster Process Notes form with each child's name along the side and the skills to look for along the top. To record more detailed information, the teacher devised a rating code and noted it in the upper left corner of the form.

Figure 16

Part of a completed Roster Process Notes form showing how a coding system helps monitor children's skills during writing

WRITERS' WORKSHOP Week of 3/17 ✔ = Proficient N = Not Yet ~ = Emerging	Independently selects topic	Establishes time and place	Recounts events in logical sequence	Includes relevant characters and details	Uses complete sentences	Uses some conventions of print
Amanthe	✔	~	~	✔	✔	✔
Bobby	~		~	N		
Devon	~	✔	✔			
Gina	~	N	✔	~		~

Sampling System®

Set Up an Organized Storage System

Teachers say that a challenge of using the Guidelines and Checklists is staying organized. Once you have decided on observation methods and tools you think will work for you, we strongly urge you to set up a system for organizing the data you collect.

We suggest creating a Teacher File for each child. At the end of the year, the Teacher File will contain the following:

- the child's Checklist
- all the observational data the teacher collects about that child
- notes from other teachers
- notes from the child's family
- health information

How you create Teacher Files is up to you. Choose a plan that works for you. Here are some ideas:

- Set up one folder for each child containing the types of records listed above

- Use a large three-ring binder with a separate section for each child. You can punch holes in the Checklist and include it, along with all the other observational data and notes, in each child's section

- Store all students' Checklists together in one folder and keep observational data for the whole class in a binder organized by domain

Above all, it is important to make this organizational system match your personal work style. If you are a visual learner, you may want to keep your Teacher Files displayed so that you can see them easily. If you are a teacher who must have a clean, orderly desk top, you'll probably want to store your Teacher Files in a file cabinet. If you already have a method that works for collecting information about individual students, there is no reason to change it just because you start to use the Work Sampling Guidelines and Checklists.

During Each Reporting Period

Four ongoing processes must be incorporated into your routines during each reporting period:

- Plan, observe, and record.
- Review Checklists periodically, making pencil ratings.
- Talk with your students about observation and expectations.
- Apply what you have learned to daily and weekly planning.

As you begin to use the Guidelines and Checklists, your focus will be on planning for observation; observing and recording; and reviewing the Checklist to narrow your observational focus. With continued use of Work Sampling, it will become increasingly valuable for you to talk with your students about the expectations on the Checklist and to use Checklist information to guide your instruction.

Plan, Observe, and Record

Although you should read the Guidelines before school begins, mastery of the Guidelines comes as a result of returning to them throughout the year as you plan curriculum and focus your observations. We recommend that you think about and plan for observation before school begins. However, making observations and recording part of your daily experience as a teacher may be one of the most challenging aspects of using the Work Sampling Guidelines and Checklists. Many teachers find that developing specific, concrete plans for observation enables them to incorporate observation and documentation effectively into their teaching. Planning for observation involves four considerations:

- Deciding what to observe
- Identifying when and where to observe
- Preparing appropriate documentation methods and tools
- Enlisting support from your colleagues

Decide What to Observe

As you plan activities and projects each week, add one question to your planning process: "How will I focus my observations this week?" This means identifying the questions you are trying to answer about individual learners and small groups of learners in your classroom.

For example, in a review of Checklists for your class, you may realize that you lack information about students' questioning and predicting skills. You may decide to schedule some open-ended science activities so you will have opportunities to observe this component of Scientific Thinking. Alternatively, your review of Checklists may reveal some very specific questions about particular students that will shape your observations for the week.

Teachers have found many ways of breaking down the task of observing all students in all seven domains into manageable parts. You may want to focus on a fifth of your class each day of the school week, alternating the day you focus on each fifth so that you are watching children on different days each week. Another method is to choose one domain, a few components, or a particular group of performance indicators, and observe all children in relation to that focus for a week.

Identify When and Where to Observe

Once you have identified a focus, review your curriculum plan for the week and decide the times of the day, routines, and activities that are most likely to reveal information that answers your questions. For example, suppose your question is, "What do the children in my class already understand about patterns?" You plan an activity or series of activities that will enable you to observe small groups of children exploring patterning. In addition, note other times when you might spontaneously see children using patterns.

It is important to remember that finding several opportunities to observe for brief periods of time is more manageable, realistic, and productive than stepping out of the action for longer periods of time.

You may prefer to record your observations when they are still fresh in your mind at the end of each day. If so, create and protect a short period of time after students leave your room for you to reflect on and record your observations.

Prepare Appropriate Documentation Methods and Tools

Your observation time can be used more efficiently if you devise documentation methods that fit the question and the setting. For example, anecdotal records on index cards work well when you have the luxury of stepping out of the action and have time to write, but a class list for jotting quick notes is more appropriate when you are facilitating group activities.

By taking into account the type of information to be gathered, the demands on your attention, and the students' activities, you will be able to determine the documentation technique best suited for recording your observations.

Enlist Support from Your Colleagues

Consider enlisting other teachers and staff members in your school to help you learn more about your students. You might ask a special subject teacher to observe for specific indicators. Or the reading specialist might give you some valuable observations related to a student's reading strategies. The school's guidance counselor could make observations as she works with a small group from your class. A parent volunteer during math work time might give you valuable information if you specify the skills and behavior to observe. Observation by others can reinforce your interpretations of students' behaviors or prompt you to look at a student in a new way.

In addition, you can work with other teachers in order to get more time for observing and organizing Checklist data. Take turns supervising recess and use the extra time to complete and organize observational records. Alternatively, you might team teach with another teacher. Then, while one of you leads a large group activity with your combined classes, the other observes and records.

Review Checklists Periodically, Making Pencil Ratings

All classroom teachers observe children continuously in the context of daily classroom activities. As a teacher who is using the Work Sampling Guidelines and Checklists, you regularly document what you see using various methods of recording. Periodically, you review the Checklists and make preliminary ratings based on the documentation you have collected.

A 5-minute monthly scanning of the Checklist and your observational data for each child is a valuable way to see what you have learned about your students and to identify the questions that remain unanswered. Making some quick, tentative pencil ratings also alerts you to the instructional needs of individual children.

As you engage in this process, what you need to find out becomes apparent and you return to the task of observing and recording with a clearer and narrower focus. You are continually asking yourself, "What do I know? What do I need to find out?" If you are unsure of the rating for a performance indicator, it probably means you need more information. You now have a new observational focus for this child.

It is not necessary to scan all of your students' Checklists at one sitting, but by the midpoint of the reporting period, it is a good idea to have reviewed all children's Checklists at least once.

Figure 17
Ongoing process of
observing, recording,
reviewing and making
Checklist ratings

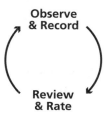

Observe
& Record

Review
& Rate

This cycle of observing and recording, reviewing and rating the Checklist, then returning to observing with a sharper focus should be repeated once or twice during each reporting period (Figure 17).

As you review the Checklists, you make ratings based on your observations using a three-point scale that describes performance mastery. The rating categories reflect the degree to which students have acquired the skill, knowledge, or behavior, and/or demonstrated the accomplishments delineated by each performance indicator described in the Guidelines and listed on the Checklist. Three types of ratings are possible:

- **Not Yet** indicates that the skill, knowledge, or behavior has not been demonstrated

- **In Process** indicates that the skill, knowledge, or behavior is emergent, and is not demonstrated consistently

- **Proficient** indicates that the skill, knowledge, or behavior is firmly within the child's range of performance

Sometimes, especially when making final ratings for the first reporting period, you will find that you are unable to rate certain performance indicators. In this case, write N/A next to the indicator on the Checklist to show that the skill has not yet been taught or an opportunity to learn this skill has not been available to students. N/A means that the child has not had the chance to demonstrate learning in this area. In contrast, "Not Yet" means that the child can not yet perform the skill, even though the child has had a chance to learn the skill.

You can review Checklists in different ways. Some teachers review each child's entire Checklist. Others review one domain at a time for all of the students in their class. To illustrate the process of reviewing and rating, let's assume a method of organization that uses one folder for each child. In this case, with information from the Guidelines in mind, the process of review would be as follows:

1 Select a child's folder.

2 Read through the observational notes.

3 Scan the Checklist. This may trigger memories of children's behaviors that you have not formally documented.

4 Using a pencil, make preliminary ratings for those performance indicators about which you have sufficient information. Expect to find indicators for which you do not have enough information to make a rating.

5 Make notations to yourself to focus your subsequent observations on these less-observed indicators.

6 Write questions, concerns, and strengths in the comments space on the front of the Checklist if it helps you organize your thoughts about students.

Talk with Students

Although children's involvement in the process of observation and Checklist completion is indirect, it is important nonetheless. Observation of children should not be kept hidden from them. When you let children know that you are observing and when you share your observations, children can become more responsible and independent learners. You can involve children in the Checklist assessment process in two ways. First, make explicit to children what they are learning and why they are learning it. Second, discuss with children what is being assessed and how the assessment process occurs.

Make the Purpose and Expectations of Learning Activities Explicit

Helping children understand the reasons and expectations for what they learn during the school year often results in a marked increase in student motivation. How you help your students understand depends on the developmental level of your students. You may want to post the Wall Chart of domains, components, and performance indicators that comes with your grade level Guidelines. If your students can read, refer them to it at appropriate times. If your students cannot yet read, you can use it when conducting class discussions about why students are learning particular skills or knowledge.

When children have a clear idea of what is being evaluated, they are likely to perform at a higher level. Too often we fail to make the criteria we intend to use for evaluation explicit to our students. They do not have the chance to make the specific type of effort needed in order to be successful. For example, a class of third grade students is given the following assignment.

Example 9

Write a report about an animal of your choice. Do research using at least two books, take notes on index cards without copying the book's exact text, write a first draft in your own words, proofread your work for spelling and punctuation, conference with a peer and then the teacher, make final revisions, and then, write a final draft. You will be evaluated on each step of this process.

If children understand these expectations in advance and are given clear guidance about how to proceed, they can be successful with the assignment.

Talk with Children About the Assessment Process

It is extremely valuable to have discussions with students about how you find out what they know. For example, you might pose the question, "Do you know why I take notes during a reading conference?" or "Why do you think I write down some of what you say during meeting time?" When children are made aware of your role as observer and recorder, they are more likely to understand why there are times when you are not available to them.

You might consider sharing the responsibility of recording student learning with your students. For example, in one classroom, the teacher assigns each child a steno pad. The child has responsibility for keeping track of the steno pad. During reading and writing conferences, the child brings the steno pad and both the teacher and the child write in it. This helps to place the responsibility for learning in the hands of the student. When completing the Checklist, the teacher reviews the observational data recorded in the steno pad along with the other types of observational data stored in the Teacher File.

Teachers have developed many ways to share the responsibility for observation with their students. One teacher, who wears a special hat when she is observing, procured a plastic "observer's hat" for her students to wear when it is their turn for this particular classroom job. She gives them a specific behavior or skill to watch for and a chart to record their observations. She adds these data to her collection of observational notes to use when completing Checklists.

Apply What You Have Learned

Observing and documenting children's learning regularly in the context of ongoing classroom activities and making preliminary Checklist ratings reveals information that will guide your decisions about curriculum and instruction. You may find that you become a more effective teacher because you are watching and listening to children closely, discovering the diverse ways children show what they know and can do, and incorporating this information into your instructional planning, thus making your teaching increasingly responsive to the children in your classroom.

Regular scanning of the Guidelines and Checklist and a review of them when planning each week enables you to keep track of whether all curriculum goals are being addressed. You can identify whether certain domains, components, or indicators are being overlooked and can structure activities to address these areas.

Additionally, this process helps ensure that you don't overlook someone. When reviewing Checklists, you may discover that you have very little observational data on a particular child. Discovering this early in the reporting period allows you to focus on that child. You will also recognize children's strengths and vulnerabilities and make plans to further their growth and learning in those areas.

Near the End of Each Reporting Period

Preparations for completing Checklists begin about two weeks before the end of each reporting period. Before you begin, you have three tasks to accomplish:

■ Review preliminary ratings.

■ Make final ratings.

■ Identify examples to share with families and to use for reporting purposes.

Review Preliminary Ratings

For each child, consult your observational notes, any other relevant information in the Teacher File, samples of the student's work, and your general knowledge about the child. Using all of this information, decide whether the tentative ratings made in pencil on the Checklist still stand or if some ratings have changed, based on more recently acquired information.

Make Final Ratings

We strongly encourage you to make final ratings on the Checklists a week or two before beginning to complete your reporting form. You are apt to feel overwhelmed if you try to make Checklist ratings and complete your reporting requirements simultaneously.

As you make the final ratings, be sure to have the Guidelines readily available so you can consult them when the meaning of an indicator is unclear or if you are unsure of expectations for a particular indicator. Take a minute to refresh your memory of the meaning of the three Checklist ratings (see page 41).

Remember that a rating reflects a child's performance based on what has been taught. A fall rating is not made based on how you expect the child to perform in the spring; it is based on how you expect the child to perform in the fall.

Make the final ratings in pen. They are now final and will not be changed. Stopping the clock in this way enables you to compare ratings from one reporting period to the next.

Identify Examples to Share with Families

As you review the Checklist data and make final ratings, highlight specific examples from your observational records that you can use to illustrate strengths and areas of concern during family-teacher conferences and for reporting purposes. You might use the space on the front cover of the Checklist to note these examples so they are easily accessible when you meet with family members and complete reports.

Chapter 4

Frequently Asked Questions About Guidelines and Checklists

Q How can I find the time to observe and record?

A First of all, it is very important to have realistic expectations about how much time you can spend observing and recording. Classrooms are busy places and even if you observed all day long, it would be impossible to record everything that goes on. However, spending a few minutes each day doing some type of observation and recording can result in a great deal of assessment data.

Sometimes teachers dread observation and recording because they think that recording observations means stepping out of the classroom activity, sitting for long periods of time, and writing lengthy anecdotal notes. We recommend that you observe both in and out of the classroom action, and that you select a recording method that best captures the information you are trying to gather. In fact, teachers who are successful observers and recorders of children's learning use multiple ways of observing and recording. They schedule observation time into their daily activities, plan who and what they will observe, and prepare methods and tools for recording in advance. With advance planning, observing a few minutes each morning and afternoon provides sufficient evidence for making Checklist ratings confidently. (Refer to the discussion beginning on page 28 for specific ideas about how to observe and record student learning.)

Q Should I set up specific situations so that I can observe the skills listed on the Checklists?

A The Work Sampling System is a curriculum-embedded assessment. This means that observation for Checklist ratings takes place in the context of regular classroom activities. Children should not be asked to perform tasks simply for the purpose of evaluation.

Effective teacher planning plays a critical role in successful observation, making it possible for you to observe all of the performance indicators on the Checklist. As you do your daily and weekly planning, consider all the different skills, knowledge, and behaviors children might exhibit during specific activities and lessons. Consider the many ways children demonstrate what they know and can do.

Teachers plan activities so that children can be introduced to or practice a skill and, of course, they hope to observe children's performance in relation to this skill during the activity. This scenario, however, does not always happen as planned. As you plan activities, be expansive in your thinking and consider all the possible skills children are learning and demonstrating. During a math activity, for example, children are likely to display many different aspects of mathematical thinking, as well as fine motor skills, language skills, and possibly skills related to the arts. This type of planning will help to make your teaching and your assessment more efficient, as illustrated in the following example.

A kindergarten teacher puts out pattern blocks during center time and introduces two-color patterns. She hopes to observe the Mathematical Thinking indicator "Recognizes, duplicates, and extends patterns." One child immediately copies the teacher's pattern and extends it. Another child, using pattern blocks for the first time, eagerly builds a wall of yellow hexagons. A third child places blocks on the table, first a red one, then a green, then a red, and then a yellow and proceeds to form the blocks into the shape of a flower.

The teacher in the above example noted that the first child copied and extended a two-color pattern. She also noted that the second child built a wall of yellow hexagons. She asked this child to describe what he had built and added his answer to her observational record. He said, "I got all yellows—they are all the same shape." His answer gave her information for the performance indicator "Sorts objects into subgroups, classifying and comparing according to a rule." Later the same day during a game of musical chairs, the child who built the wall commented that the chairs were set up in a pattern. Children demonstrate what they are learning in many ways, though as teachers, we are often tuned into only those demonstrations we expect to see.

Effective observation calls for widening your focus and observing more broadly, in different situations, at different times of the day, and when children are interacting with different materials. If you are having difficulty observing particular indicators, consider the following questions:

♦ Have these children been provided with adequate opportunities to learn this skill?

♦ Is this skill one that I have addressed in my teaching?

♦ Have I observed for this skill in many different situations?

♦ Have I given students different ways to express their knowledge?

q How do Guidelines and Checklists help me with curriculum planning?

> **A** Developmental Guidelines and Checklists can help with curriculum planning in three different ways.

> ♦ The Guidelines remind you of the breadth of the curriculum. They address seven domains and include a wide range of activities typical of developmentally appropriate classrooms.

> ♦ Systematic observation and documentation highlight areas of the curriculum that you may be overlooking.

> ♦ Carefully observing children and documenting what you see gives you in-depth knowledge of children. This helps you plan instruction that is more responsive to individual children as well as to the class as a whole.

Because the Guidelines and Checklists emphasize continuous progress across ages and grades, you gain a sense of what your students can do now as well as where they need to go in the future. Familiarity with the Guidelines and Checklists can help both you and your students set learning goals.

Q How can I be sure that my observations are fair?

A To make a fair determination about whether a child knows or can do something, it is essential that you observe the child more than once and in more than one situation.

For the assessment to be fair, students should be evaluated only on indicators that have already been addressed in the classroom. It is unfair to hold children responsible for demonstrating skills, knowledge, and behaviors that have not been taught. Moreover, bear in mind that children may have certain skills, even if they do not exhibit them in the particular contexts you have chosen. It is the teacher's responsibility to provide varied experiences within the classroom in which all students are likely to demonstrate their achievements and accomplishments.

Using an observational assessment requires you to collect factual data before making judgments. People have a tendency, however, to form impressions quickly. For example, when you have difficulty with a particular child's behavior, it is not uncommon to generalize your impressions to all encounters with that child. A child who is extremely talkative or who tends to dominate social interactions with peers may be strong in mathematics or a very talented artist, but the child's behavior may interfere with your ability to observe his strengths. Observing as fairly as possible requires that teachers look at all children through the same lens. We recommend that you get in the habit of reserving judgment. Try to observe what the child is doing now, and how the child is approaching this task, rather than how the child may have behaved or performed in a very different situation at a different time.

Q How can I know that my Checklist ratings are valid and reliable?

A The Work Sampling Guidelines provide a set of criteria for performance based on national and state standards and child development research. The Guidelines also provide teachers with a set of shared expectations for children's learning. Your Checklist ratings will be valid and reliable only when you interpret your observations and make ratings consistent with the expectations described in the Guidelines, rather than ratings based on personal opinions. If you are having difficulty making a child's ratings, it may be helpful to discuss them with a colleague.

Q Why is it necessary to record observations?

A Observational records are the evidence or the data upon which evaluations are based. The documentation process in the Work Sampling System has two steps. The first step is the informal note-taking or data-gathering that you do on a regular basis. The second consists of the ratings you make on the Work Sampling Checklist in response to your informal observational notes. Recording observations is important for four reasons.

♦ Written records help you monitor what children know and can do. They remind you of a child's strengths and weaknesses.

♦ Written records collected over time enable you to see patterns in behaviors and approaches to learning.

♦ You can use your observations of children to plan instructional activities that are more responsive to children's interests and needs.

♦ Recorded observations provide evidence to support your judgments in the assessment process.

Without careful documentation, the reliability of Checklist ratings decreases and the validity of your judgments is compromised.

Q Is it possible for a rating to change from "Proficient" to "In Process" from the fall to the spring?

A Yes. Although the Guidelines describe developmental expectations for performance indicators in broad terms, you complete Checklists based on your expectations for a particular time of year. For example, when evaluating a child's performance for the Checklist in November, you consider what you have taught and your expectations of children at that time, and then make your ratings accordingly. A child who was using several reading strategies in the fall of second grade to read simple books might be rated "Proficient" on the Checklist because that was the fall expectation. By spring, however, the expectation is that children will be reading more difficult material. If the child is still reading only simple books, his rating at this time will be "In Process."

Q Are Checklists sent home?

> **A** Checklists are not designed to be sent home. They are written in language for teachers. However, parents always have access to the Checklist should they request it, and you may wish to use the Checklists during conferences to help families understand how their child is doing in a particular domain.

Q Can I use the Checklist during parent-teacher conferences?

> **A** Although reviewing the entire Checklist during a conference would take too much time, sometimes teachers find it helpful to refer to particular sections of the Checklist as a way to offer specific information about a child's strengths or weaknesses or to illustrate a rating on the Summary Report. Keep in mind, though, that Checklists are written in professional language and that the amount and organization of information recorded there is complex and may be overwhelming to a parent in the context of a brief conference.

Q How can specialists or special subjects teachers be involved in completing Checklists?

> **A** Specialists can contribute a great deal to the richness and detail of the Checklist. The more information you have about students, the more accurate your assessment. Collaboration and dialogue among all of the adults who work with a child will enhance accuracy. The Guidelines should be shared with special subject and resource teachers so that they can channel appropriate information to you. Specialists can give the child's primary teacher observational records and/or work samples relevant to their subject areas, all of which can be used to inform the Work Sampling Checklist. Having conferences with special subject teachers can be a useful way to gather this information. An optional Special Subject Report form (described in Chapter 4) is available for use by specialists. (For further discussion of these issues, see Chapter 6.)

Q Why are Checklists filled out three times during the school year?

A Children grow and change at different rates. Their growth often occurs quite rapidly. As children change, you form new images of their achievements based on their current performance, and you may forget some of the details of their prior performances. Only by noting a child's specific performance at one point in time can you accurately assess the child's progress later. For this reason, we advocate a three-times-per-year framework for assessment so that the child's profile of skills and knowledge in one collection period can be compared with her profile in an earlier period. This facilitates assessment of progress and provides a chance to record change in performance.

Q What happens to the Checklist at the end of the year?

A We recommend that you include the Checklist in the child's school file at the end of the year so that it can be reviewed by the child's next teacher. At the beginning of the next year, the new teacher has the opportunity to scan the spring ratings on the Checklists and obtain a starting point for review and instruction. This is particularly helpful given that the Work Sampling System is continuous from one grade to the next.

Although parents have legal access to all information about their children, the Checklists are not intended to be sent home at the end of the year because they have been written with educators, rather than parents, in mind.

Q How long does it take to learn how to use the Guidelines and Checklists?

A After the first two collection periods, most teachers have internalized much of the information included in the Guidelines for the grade levels they teach. Although they may occasionally refer back to the Guidelines, they do it much less frequently than earlier in the school year.

The greatest difficulty teachers have in completing the Checklists is integrating the observing, recording, reviewing, and rating cycle into their daily schedules. This process is facilitated by the following:

♦ Observing and recording selectively, instead of trying to document everything all the time

♦ Planning when, how, and what will be observed each week

♦ Finding documentation strategies that feel comfortable

Q How long does it take to complete the Checklist?

A If you review and rate the Checklist in an ongoing way, scanning the Checklist takes less than five minutes, and reviewing all information collected in order to make final ratings takes about 15 minutes per child. If rating particular indicators is difficult or time consuming, you probably need more information about the child, and should continue to observe.

Q Which Checklist should I use for children above or below grade-level expectations?

A Development in children is rarely even. Many children who function above or below grade-level do not do so in all domains. Rather, they may be at grade-level for some domains while being above or below expectations in others. For example, a child who is very mature verbally may be less so socially. Because of this natural variability, we recommend that you use as a starting point the Checklist that corresponds to the child's age/grade level.

For those children who are functioning very differently from expectations, perhaps a child with a disability, information from the Omnibus Guidelines can be used to increase your understanding of the areas in which the child is above or below grade level. The examples in the Guidelines will help you to modify your instructional plans to reflect the child's skills and knowledge in all of the domains. The Summary Report should also be used to address the areas in which the child is performing above or below grade-level. Particularly for the child who is working below grade-level, it is important to describe what the child can do, not only the child's areas of difficulty. (Refer to Chapter 6 for more information on using Checklists with children with special needs.)

Q My school has four reporting periods. Can I still use the Checklist?

A Although the Checklist is designed to reflect three reporting periods, you can still use the Checklist with your four marking periods. For your fourth period, just make your rating in the margin next to the "spring" block. You might want to change the labels on the columns from "fall," "winter," and "spring," to "1," "2," "3," and "4."

Q How can I possibly observe everything that is going on in the classroom?

A You cannot observe everything that happens in your classroom. To maximize the effectiveness of your observations, it is best that they be planned and focused. Reviewing the Guidelines in conjunction with weekly curriculum planning can help provide that focus. Devising a plan about whom and what to observe as part of weekly planning makes the task of observation more systematic. Some ideas include observing

♦ four or five pupils each day

♦ a group of students for the week

♦ one domain for several days

♦ a few components of one domain during a lesson

Becoming a skilled observer takes time and practice. Teachers usually find it beneficial to try out several methods of observation and recording, then talk them over with colleagues and revise their plans before they create a method that reflects their personal style. Above all, it is important to try to establish a routine in which you observe and document classroom activities on a regular and consistent basis.

Q Should I have a documented observation for every performance indicator on the Checklist?

A Absolutely not. There are two reasons why documented observations for each performance indicator are unnecessary. First, each time you observe your students, you gain information that provides data for multiple performance indicators on the Checklist. For example, Ms. Stevens records two anecdotal notes about Raymond, a first grader, during one week in October (Examples 10 and 11). Each anecdote provided her with information about several performance indicators. To illustrate, we have listed the performance indicators that are informed by Ms. Stevens' observation below each anecdote.

EXAMPLE 10

1. *10/7 choose to wk w/manips at choice, many patterns, organized design, some symmetry*

Related performance indicators:

I A 2—Shows initiative and self-direction.

I B 2—Uses materials purposefully and respectfully.

III C 2—Makes, copies, and extends patterns.

III D 2—Explores and solves spatial problems using manipulatives and drawings.

EXAMPLE 11

2. *10/9 during QR (quiet reading) brings me Zoobook on eagles: "This is amazing." We read a few pgs tog, listens intently to me, studies pictures, he reads 1 pg, uses picture cues, sounds out wds.*

Related performance indicators:

I C 1—Shows eagerness and curiosity as a learner.

I C 2—Sustains attention to work over a period of time.

II B 1—Speaks clearly and conveys ideas effectively.

II C 5—Comprehends and interprets fiction and non-fiction text.

II C 1—Shows interest in books and reading.

II C 4—Uses strategies to construct meaning from print.

The second reason each performance indicator may not have a recorded observation is that you may have observed a child performing certain skills so frequently that you can rely on your memory.

Q How are the Guidelines and Checklists used in multi-age classrooms?

A Work Sampling fits well with multi-age classrooms because of the emphasis in these classrooms on the continuum of children's development. By examining all six levels of an indicator presented in the Omnibus Guidelines, you gain an understanding of what comes before and after each grade level indicator. Although the Omnibus Guidelines present several levels of development at once, the Checklists do not.

Teachers of multi-age groups use several different Checklists to reflect the developmental range their students represent. Thus, if you have a class of seven and eight year olds, you would complete second grade Checklists for the seven year olds, and the third grade Checklists for the eight year olds. Because of the consistency of the domains, components, and many of the indicators across grade levels, you do not have to learn entirely new information for each age represented in your classroom. The rationales and examples describe the differences from one grade level to another. The Omnibus Guidelines supports your instructional planning by enabling you to quickly identify similarities and differences among age levels and to move easily between grade levels (for further discussion see Chapter 6).

Q Can the Guidelines and Checklists be customized to meet the requirements of a particular state or district?

A The fourth edition of Work Sampling has been revised to conform to a wide range of local, state, and national standards, as well as to the standards and expectations of a variety of national curriculum groups and organizations. Nevertheless, some states, districts, and major educational providers (e.g., Head Start) have their own set of standards which do not correspond specifically to the Work Sampling components and indicators. In some cases, with the publisher's permission, it is possible to revise the Work Sampling materials so that they are more closely aligned with these standards. More information about customization is available from the publisher, Pearson Early Learning.

CHAPTER 5

Reporting Children's Performance and Progress

THE WORK SAMPLING DEVELOPMENTAL GUIDELINES AND CHECKLISTS help teachers gather rich evidence of student performance in seven curricular domains. Through observing children's behaviors, recording observations, and making Checklist ratings, teachers learn a great deal about their students. The Guidelines and Checklists help teachers understand how their students perform specific skills, acquire knowledge, and approach learning. In addition, they enable teachers to keep track of specific examples and anecdotes that illustrate each student's classroom performance. To share all of this information with parents would go beyond the 15-minute conferences most districts and programs usually schedule. Therefore, in order to communicate this information to families and administrators, it is important to summarize it. The rich documentation collected with the Guidelines and Checklists must be condensed into a manageable amount of information that reflects each student's learning during the reporting period so that it can be shared with families.

Reasons for Reporting

In addition to reporting information to families efficiently, there are at least three reasons to integrate your observations and Checklist ratings into an overall evaluation.

Presenting an Integrated Picture of the "Whole Child"

Completing an overall evaluation gives teachers time to reflect on each of their students and to create an individualized profile of each student's achievement in the seven Work Sampling domains. When you make Checklist ratings throughout the reporting period you focus on specific skills and sets of accomplishments. In contrast, evaluation at the end of the reporting period allows you to combine these skills and accomplishments in order to view the "whole child."

Guiding Instructional Planning

The process of synthesizing and summarizing knowledge about students helps teachers plan curriculum and instruction. As you review your observations and ratings, you gain insight that can help you individualize instruction. At the end of a reporting period, after you have written reports for your entire class, you will have a new perspective on how to meet the needs of your students and on whether your classroom practices address the entire span of the curriculum.

Providing Information to Administrators about Student Achievement

Teachers need ways to communicate their students' academic accomplishments easily and efficiently. Your summary of student learning is useful to administrators who want to know about student achievement in a particular classroom or school.

Information to Include in Reports

When teachers report to families at the end of the reporting period, their goal is to present an overall evaluation of children's performance and progress across the curriculum. Below, we clarify the meaning of the terms evaluation, performance, and progress.

Evaluation

Evaluation consists of judging how closely something compares to a standard. When teachers rate performance indicators on the Work Sampling Checklist, they are evaluating each student's performance against criteria for performance described in the Guidelines. These expectations are based on national standards, information from curricular organizations, and child development research. Children's performances in school are compared to these criteria, not to the performance of other students in the classroom.

At the end of each reporting period, teachers engage in another type of evaluation. They evaluate each student's overall performance for the reporting period. In other words, rather than assessing particular writing skills, teachers make judgments about each student's writing performance in general. This information is recorded on a reporting form and then shared with families.

In addition to describing what children have learned and how they have progressed, the overall evaluation should give some information about each student's approach to learning. Describing how students learn is helpful to the child's next teacher, as well as to the child's family.

Performance

Performance describes the current level of a child's behavior, skills, and accomplishments at a particular point in time. When you evaluate a child's performance, you are examining the student's skills over the course of a reporting period and comparing them to a standard for children of that age. The Developmental Guidelines focus specifically on performance in seven curricular domains.

Progress

Progress refers to growth or change over time. It is evaluated by comparing a child's performance from one time period to another. When you evaluate a child's progress, you are comparing the child's current performance with his past performance, rather than comparing his current performance to an external standard or to other students' progress.

Reporting Methods

After making Checklist ratings, you have several different ways to present an overall evaluation of children's performance and progress. Three primary reporting methods are:

1 Using your current report card
2 Modifying your current report card or creating a new one
3 Using the Work Sampling Report To Parents

Each of these options will be discussed below, along with suggestions for deciding which option to use.

Using Your Current Report Card

Many teachers observe their students using the Work Sampling Guidelines and Checklists and summarize this information using their current report card. This option works best in the following situations:

1 When only a single teacher or a few teachers are using the Guidelines and Checklists, they may not have the authority to change their reporting method. Usually the choice of reporting form is determined by the school, program, or district. Therefore, if the Guidelines and Checklists are not used school-wide, it is likely that the current report card will be used at the end of each reporting period.

2 Some programs use a report card that already reflects the seven domains of the Checklist. In this case, teachers may add comments about progress, but use their existing evaluation system to rate children's performance in each domain.

3 Sometimes teachers want to pilot or try out the Guidelines and Checklists before making changes in their overall reporting system. During this trial period they may continue using their existing report card. At the end of the trial period, if they are satisfied with the process of observing their students and completing Checklists, they can then decide on the format for the overall evaluative report.

Modifying Your Current Report Card Or Creating A New One

If a school or program staff decide that their current report card does not accurately reflect student performance, progress, and the information acquired from the Guidelines and Checklists, they may decide to change their report card or design a new one. Thinking about the following questions will help you design a form that works well with the Checklist.

1 What do you want to evaluate?
   For example:

   - performance in the Work Sampling domains and components
   - progress from one reporting period to another
   - additional domains or components identified by your school or district (e.g., technology)

2 What do you want to use to evaluate students?
   - ratings
   - narrative comments
   - a combination of ratings and comments

3 If you use ratings, what type of rating system will you use?
   For example:

   - words (Pass, Fail; Needs improvement, Satisfactory, Advanced, etc.)
   - letter grades
   - numerical ratings (1, 2, 3; 85%, etc.)

4 What identifying information should be included on the form?
   For example:

   - child's name
   - child's date of birth
   - grade level
   - teacher's name
   - school name
   - reporting period
   - student ID number
   - date report completed

5 What other information does your district require?
For example:

- days absent, present, or tardy
- parental signature and/or comments
- child's signature and/or comments
- other

By answering these questions, a school or program faculty can begin to design a form that reflects the Work Sampling Checklist, meets the needs of their district, and communicates evaluative information clearly and directly to families.

Using the Work Sampling Report To Parents

The third method for reporting is to use the Work Sampling Report To Parents. This Report is designed to reflect the information on the Checklist and to supplement it with teachers' comments about each domain. The form is produced on carbonless paper in three copies: one for the family, one for the teacher, and one for the child's cumulative school file. The form and its use are explained in the next section.

Standards of Comparison

The Work Sampling Report To Parents relies upon two different standards of comparison. When you evaluate a student's *performance* based on the Checklist, you compare the student's performance to national standards or expectations for children of a particular age or grade. These external age- or grade-related expectations are described in the Developmental Guidelines.

When you evaluate a student's *progress* you use information from the Checklist to compare the student's present performance to the student's past performance. In this case the standard of comparison is internal—the child's own performance.

Another way to understand the two different standards of comparison is to think of the performance column as comparing the child's performance to expectations for *all children* and the progress column as comparing this child today to *this child* at an earlier time.

The Work Sampling Report To Parents

Current reporting period (fall, winter, or year-end)

Child's identifying information and attendance record

List of domains and components

CHILD	AGE	**The Work Sampling. Report To Parents**
SCHOOL/PROGRAM		FALL ☐
TEACHER	DATE	WINTER ☐
ATTENDANCE: DAYS PRESENT	DAYS ABSENT	SPRING ☐

DOMAINS & COMPONENTS	PERFORMANCE				PROGRESS		CHILD'S DEVELOPMENT: Note special strengths and talents; explain how Partially Proficient and Needs Development areas will be addressed. Comment on Progress.
	Advanced	Proficient	Partially Proficient	Needs Development	As Expected	Less Than Expected	
I Personal & Social Development							
Self concept							
Self control							
Approaches to learning							
Interaction with others							
Social problem-solving							
II Language & Literacy							
Listening							
Speaking							
Reading							
Writing							
Research (3-5)							
III Mathematical Thinking							
Mathematical processes							
Number and operations							
Patterns, relationships, and functions							
Geometry and spatial relations							
Measurement							
Data collection and probability (K-5)							
IV Scientific Thinking							
Inquiry							
Physical science (K-5)							
Life science (K-5)							
Earth science (K-5)							
V Social Studies							
People, past and present							
Human interdependence							
Citizenship and government							
People and where they live							
VI The Arts							
Expression and representation							
Understanding and appreciation							
VII Physical Development & Health							
Gross motor development							
Fine motor development							
Personal health and safety							

SEE REVERSE FOR HOW TO READ THIS REPORT
4th Edition © 2003 Pearson Education, Inc., publishing as Pearson Early Learning, New York, NY 10036. All Rights Reserved.

WHITE – FAMILY   YELLOW – OFFICE   PINK – CLASSROOM TEACHER

Performance ratings are made for each component based on Checklist ratings

Progress ratings are made based on change in the child's performance from one reporting period to another (optional in fall reporting period)

General comments illustrate performance and progress ratings

Information on back of the report explains the ratings to teachers and families unfamiliar with The Work Sampling Report

Completing the Work Sampling Report To Parents

About two weeks before the end of each reporting period or before conferences are held, begin to complete Reports on your students. By the time you begin, you should have already organized your observational data and rated your students' Checklists. Then, use the following steps as a guide to completing your Reports.

- Get organized and fill in identifying information
- Evaluate performance
- Evaluate progress
- Write comments
- Proofread reports
- Share with families

Get Organized and Fill In Identifying Information

Before beginning work on a student's Report, collect and review all of the information you have about that child. This usually consists of the following:

- Observation notes
- Developmental Checklist
- Information from the child's family
- Information from specialists
- Previous Work Sampling Reports To Parents
- Other information (e.g., running records, individualized reading inventories)

Teachers use a variety of strategies to complete their Reports. Some teachers complete each student's entire Report before going on to the next student. Others fill in everyone's identifying information, then rate performance for all of their students, and finally rate progress for all students. Still other teachers completely evaluate one domain for their entire class, making ratings and writing comments, before moving on to evaluating another domain for all their students. Regardless of how you organize this task, it is a good idea to divide the work into small parts spread over two weeks.

Evaluate Performance

As defined earlier, performance describes the current level of a child's behavior, skills, and accomplishments. When you evaluate a child's performance, you are examining the student's skills within each component during a reporting period and comparing them to an external standard for children of that age. Ask yourself, "How does this child's current level of performance compare to expectations for all children of this age or grade?"

Then make one of the following four ratings: Advanced, Proficient, Partially Proficient, or Needs Development. These ratings can be converted into those used in the federal Title I program (see p. 84).

To translate Checklist ratings into an overall evaluation of performance, first review the Checklist ratings one component at a time for the reporting period you are evaluating. For example, in the winter, examine all the winter ratings of performance indicators within the component of Writing. Then, for each component, examine the pattern of ratings and determine the overall evaluation by using the chart below.

CHECKLIST RATINGS	PERFORMANCE RATINGS ON REPORT TO PARENTS
All performance indicators within a component are rated Proficient. The student's work exceeds grade level expectations.	"Advanced"
All or most performance indicators within a component are rated Proficient; none is rated Not Yet. The student's work meets grade level expectations.	"Proficient"
All or nearly all performance indicators within a component are rated In Process; a few may be rated Proficient and/or Not Yet. The student's work is inconsistent and does not always meet grade level expectations.	"Partially Proficient"
Nearly all performance indicators within a component are rated Not Yet; a few may be rated In Process, but none is rated Proficient. The student's work does not meet grade level expectations.	"Needs Development"

This framework shows how to translate ratings of individual Performance Indicators on the Checklist into more global ratings of Components on the Work Sampling Report To Parents. Remember that to evaluate performance, you must compare each student's performance to expectations for all children as identified in the Developmental Guidelines.

Evaluate Progress

Progress refers to growth or change over time. When you evaluate a child's progress, you are comparing the child's current performance with that child's previous performance. The progress rating does not involve comparing a particular student's progress with an external measure. Instead, progress is evaluated within the context of each child's work; the child is only compared with him or herself.

For the progress rating, you review Checklist ratings from the current reporting period for each component and compare them to the past reporting period. Because children do not develop at the same rate, the standard for rating progress is internal to each child. Ask yourself, "Compared to the earlier performance, has this student made expected progress?"

The progress rating incorporates information across reporting periods. The ratings are: As Expected and Less Than Expected.

Because children within the same early childhood classroom may differ from one another developmentally by as much as two years, it is impossible to establish definitive standards for rating progress. Therefore, you must use your knowledge of child development and your teaching experience as guides when considering how to evaluate a child's growth since the previous reporting period.

To evaluate progress, compare Checklist ratings within each component from one reporting period to an earlier period. Use the following guide to facilitate this process:

CHECKLIST RATINGS	PROGRESS RATINGS ON THE REPORT TO PARENTS
The child has made adequate or more than adequate progress from one reporting period to another	"As Expected"
The child has shown no progress from an earlier reporting period, or has made very limited gains.	"Less Than Expected"

FALL PROGRESS RATING The progress rating at the end of the fall reporting period is optional. However, teachers sometimes observe enough growth from the beginning of school to the end of the fall reporting period to feel comfortable making a progress rating. This decision is left to the individual teacher and may vary from child to child within a classroom and from domain to domain for each child.

RELATIONSHIP BETWEEN PERFORMANCE AND PROGRESS RATINGS Performance and progress ratings are not always identical. Children may perform quite proficiently, yet still not show growth. The opposite may also be true. For example, the performance of a student with special needs may be delayed in several domains. However, this child's progress may be quite impressive when compared with his previous performance within a particular domain. Similarly, a second grader who is unable to identify letters in September but who can sound out and read simple words in March, may be rated "Partially Proficient" for performance on the Checklist in Literature and Reading, but demonstrate progress that is "Above Expectations." These differences in ratings are explained by the different standards for progress and performance.

After completing the performance and progress ratings for each component, it is time to write comments.

Write Comments

Comments are included on the Work Sampling Report To Parents to individualize and personalize the Report for each student. Although two children may have identical ratings, it is unlikely that both children will have exactly the same skills and knowledge or the same approach to learning. Moreover, even if two children have fairly similar skills, they probably do not demonstrate their skills and knowledge in the same manner. For example, three third graders, all rated as "Proficient" in Literature and Reading, may use strategies to extract meaning from print equally well. However, one child reads voraciously and uses books to discover information about topics of personal interest, another reads mostly for pleasure and escape, and the third reads efficiently but seems to take little enjoyment from the experience. The comments on the Report allow you to describe not only the child's skills, but also how the child demonstrates those skills. Comments enrich the information provided by the performance and progress ratings and allow you to explain and describe each child's performance in a detailed, individualized way.

As you write comments, consider the following issues:

AUDIENCE The child's family is the primary audience for the Work Sampling Report To Parents. Your knowledge of a child's family will help determine the specific content of the Report, how much to write, how much detail to give, and what the focus of the comments should be.

PURPOSE The purpose of the Report is to communicate constructive and clear information about child performance and progress in easily understood language.

CONTENT Writing comments gives you a chance to describe the child's overall achievement within each domain and/or to explain particular ratings. Your comments should highlight the child's unique learning characteristics, interests, and accomplishments.

Comments allow you to explain a "Partially Proficient" performance rating or a "Less Than Expected" progress rating. To help families understand their child's difficulties, give specific information. Especially for a child who is struggling in a particular domain, it is important to describe the child's progress, even if his performance does not meet expectations for children of his age or grade.

Two other issues should be considered when preparing comments:

- *Individuality.* When determining how much to write, consider whether or not you have conveyed each child's individuality rather than simply listed the child's skills and knowledge. An effective Report communicates each child's personality and approach to learning. The Report should give the reader a sense of who the child is as a learner. Adding specific examples of behavior and language that are drawn from your observation records gives the family a more complete understanding of their child as a learner.

- *Family participation.* Many families want to participate in their child's learning. Suggestions for concrete ways that the family can work with the child at home to further his or her educational goals may also be included in the Report. Asking families to work with you in helping students acquire particular concepts or skills shows that you value their involvement.

HOW MUCH TO WRITE The length of the comments is influenced by the type of information you want the family to have. It is unnecessary and overly time-consuming to address every indicator and component in your comments. Whether or not the Report will be given to the family at a conference will also influence the length of the Report. How much to write is best answered by asking yourself whether you have conveyed the essential information about this child's learning in a domain. If the answer is yes, then you have written enough. If you feel you need more space than is allotted on the Report form, attach separate pages.

LANGUAGE Although content is very important, how that content is communicated is critical. Below are tips for writing comments that will help you communicate constructive information about child performance and progress in easily understood language.

- *Be specific and descriptive.* Comments are most meaningful to families when they are specific and descriptive, rather than abstract and vague. In anticipation of completing your Reports, we recommend that you note specific examples from your observational records that you may want to use in your comments. Be sure to avoid using educational jargon.

- *Use language directly from the Developmental Guidelines.* Teachers may find it helpful to use actual words or phrases from the Guidelines. If you incorporate language from the Guidelines, however, it is important that you add specific examples unique to the child, so that the report retains a sense of the child's individuality.

- *Individualize the comments.* Use the child's own words and describe specific events. This personalizes comments in a very effective way and makes the Report more meaningful to families.

- *Be positive.* The comments on the Report should be positive in tone. The should never be angry or negative. It is best to state what a child can do, not only what she is unable to do. A report that is positive in tone does not mislead the family about the student's performance, or gloss over areas of difficulty, but leaves families hopeful about their child's future accomplishments.

- *Be respectful.* Your comments should demonstrate respect for children, their approaches to learning, and their accomplishments. Be careful about word choice and avoid the use of colloquialisms or slang that may be misinterpreted. Words such as "bossy," "sulky," and "stubborn" are easy to misinterpret and should not appear in reports.

Proofread Reports

All reports should be grammatically correct and free of spelling errors. After you have completed all your students' Reports, take time to review them. Make sure that the Reports you completed last have the same level of detail as those you finished on the first day. Check that your tone has remained positive, and that you have communicated the most important information about each child to their families. Sometimes it is helpful to exchange Reports with a colleague to make sure that you have not omitted any ratings, that your spelling is accurate, and that your comments are constructive.

Share with Families

The Work Sampling Report To Parents is best discussed with the family at a conference, rather than sent home without personal contact. The conferences will increase your confidence that parents understand the Report, and will give parents an opportunity to ask questions, contribute information, and share their concerns. Some teachers send the Work Sampling Report To Parents home and then ask parents to bring it with them to the conference. This allows the family time to read the Report and to formulate questions privately before coming in for the conference. Family members with limited reading skills will need the Report read to them during the family-teacher conference.

Although ideally all three Reports should be discussed at a conference we realize that this is not always possible. Nevertheless, it is important that the first Report of the school year be shared at a conference. This gives you an opportunity to explain the format of the Report to family members and to establish personal contact. If there are two conference times during the year, we recommend sharing the first two Reports at conferences and sending the final Report home without a conference.

CONFERENCE PREPARATION Conferences are most successful when teachers are prepared and families can participate actively. Because conferences are generally quite brief, you have to prepare in advance to make the most of the short time you have together. Most teachers structure the conference around the Report, and use examples of student work to illustrate important points. Although the Checklist is primarily designed for use by the teacher, it may be shown to parents to help clarify a student's performance within a particular domain.

CONDUCTING THE CONFERENCE After the Report is completed and before the conference, identify the most important points to communicate in a face-to-face situation. Some teachers create a structure by focusing on strengths, concerns, and plans. They may make brief notes about points to highlight and may select examples of student work to illustrate important points.

At the beginning of the conference, elicit information from the family to acknowledge the unique knowledge and perspective they bring to the conference. Some questions that you might want to ask include:

- What does the child like to do at home?
- How does the family perceive the child's personality and strengths?
- What special interests does the child pursue at home?
- What does the child say about school?
- What are the family's goals for the child this year?

In addition to asking these kinds of questions, the family should also be given ample opportunity to ask questions about their child's educational program and performance at school.

Involve Students in Overall Evaluation and Reporting

The Work Sampling Guidelines and Checklists lend themselves to student involvement in evaluation. When teachers talk with students about why they are observing, and when they share the Checklist with their students, they are preparing their students to be involved in evaluation. As much as possible, students should be encouraged to partici-pate in the reporting process. Student involvement helps make assess-ment less mysterious and anxiety-provoking. Rather than viewing eval-uation as something external to themselves, students can begin to view evaluation as part of the learning process and as something they can control.

Student involvement with reporting and evaluation can take several dif-ferent forms. It is critical that evaluation become a part of the learning process, and that students not feel that evaluation is a secret, or only of concern to parents and teachers. Consider the following possibilities for student involvement:

ASK STUDENTS TO REVIEW THEIR WORK AND COMMENT ON IT As the end of a reporting period nears, you may ask students to review the work they did during the past 8 to 12 weeks. Students may select particular items that they want you to share with their family. Or they may write a para-graph describing their progress and identifying a few personal learning goals for the next reporting period.

ARRANGE INDIVIDUAL MEETINGS WITH STUDENTS BEFORE FAMILY-TEACHER CON-FERENCES Some teachers meet with every student before the family-teacher conference. The teacher reviews the reporting form with the student and asks her if there is any information she specifically wants communicated to her family.

INVITE STUDENTS TO PARTICIPATE IN CONFERENCES One advantage to asking students to be part of the conference is that students do not feel that what occurs at the conference is a secret shared only by adults. By par-ticipating in conferences, they are able to see how important their edu-cation is to their family and to their teacher.

ENCOURAGE STUDENT-LED CONFERENCES Student-led conferences represent a very high level of student participation in reporting and in family-teacher conferences. It requires advance preparation by both you and your students. You may discuss the student's work and progress with him and arrive at a consensus regarding information that should be shared. Offer students an opportunity to role-play their conference role with each other before the conference. Students also can select work that illustrates their learning.

At the conference, the student introduces his family to you. Conferences may be scheduled to allow time for the student to give his family a tour of the classroom or school. When the conference begins, the student shows his work. After the child has had an opportunity to talk about the work, the teacher also adds comments. The conference concludes with the teacher, student, and family setting learning goals for the next reporting period.

Conclusion

Whether you use your current report card, modify it to create a new reporting form, or adopt the Work Sampling Report To Parents, it is important to give families an overall evaluation of their child at the end of each reporting period. This helps parents focus on the important elements of their child's achievement without getting caught up in or overwhelmed by issues concerning their child's specific skills and knowledge.

Completing an overall evaluation gives you an opportunity to reflect on each student's learning. As you prepare Reports, you can integrate what you have learned from the Developmental Checklists with your own knowledge of child development and make evaluative decisions about each student's performance and progress. At the end of this process, you will have additional information to help you plan instruction for your class as a whole, as well as insights about how to work with individual students. You will also have critically important information available in a summary form to share with school administrators.

Whatever path you choose, evaluative information should be accurate, presented fairly, and leave families and children informed and optimistic about future learning. We believe that the Work Sampling Guidelines and Checklists, in combination with an overall evaluative report, will help you and your students achieve your goals and experience educational excellence.

Chapter 6

Using Guidelines and Checklists with Varied Groups of Students

THIS CHAPTER DESCRIBES MODIFICATIONS AND CHANGES IN EMPHASIS when using the Developmental Guidelines and Checklists in different classroom contexts.

Preschool and Kindergarten

Completion of the Checklists does not differ markedly in preschool classrooms. However, when children attend preschool or kindergarten half days for five days a week, or two or three mornings or afternoons per week, teachers cannot expect to do the same amount of observation and recording for each of their students as a teacher who spends all day with one class of children.

In this situation, you may decide to complete Checklists in fewer than seven domains. In addition, it is important that you establish reasonable expectations about the amount of observational data you can record and collect. Since the goal of using the Guidelines and Checklists is to get to know your students in order to evaluate their work and plan effectively for instruction, we encourage you to consider carefully how much is necessary to document in order to know your students well.

Older Elementary Students

Older elementary students (third, fourth, and fifth graders) can take an active role in all aspects of the assessment process. Unlike children in earlier grades, third, fourth, and fifth graders can begin to think and talk about their learning and reflect on it. They can more easily discuss their work, understand and develop evaluative criteria, set personal goals, and evaluate their performance and progress.

Students in third, fourth, and fifth grade can understand what they are expected to learn and can participate in conversations about their own learning. Because children of these ages can understand the idea that there are categories (domains and components) of learning, and that there are specific skills and concepts they are expected to learn, you can introduce them to the structure and organization of the Checklist. For example, a fourth grader can understand that one area of study is mathematical thinking and that there are different units of study within the broader category. In addition, the student can begin to recognize that he has greater understanding of number concepts than spatial relationships. You may want to display the wall chart in a prominent place and use it as the basis for goal setting discussions.

Many teachers of third, fourth, and fifth graders use daily journals or learning logs with their students. At the close of an activity or at the end of the day they have students reflect on their work and their learning, sometimes with a specific focus. For example, a teacher might ask students to reflect on how they collaborated with others during a science investigation, or to describe the strategies they used to solve a set of math problems. Other teachers suggest that their students reflect on reading and writing conferences with the teacher and with peers. Students' written reflections provide additional observational data for teachers to use when completing the Checklists.

We strongly encourage teachers of all age groups to talk with children about expectations for work. However, older children should be encouraged to engage in detailed and meaningful discussions about the criteria for quality work. Many teachers begin these discussions with the topic of writing, because it is concrete and accessible to students, asking them to generate a list of the characteristics of a good piece of writing. At the outset of the year the list generated by a group of third graders may be superficial and include only the following: stay on one topic, have a beginning, middle, and end, and be interesting. Writing lessons throughout the year can support students' acquisition of increasingly complex characteristics such as voice, mechanics, and organization. As students acquire an understanding of evaluative criteria, they can begin to develop rubrics for evaluating work. A rubric is a scoring tool that describes levels of accomplishment. Having developed evaluation criteria, they can be more thoughtful judges of their own work and the work of others.

When students have been involved in discussions of evaluation criteria, they have a greater interest in reviewing and evaluating their own performance and setting goals for future performance. As students develop their own goals for learning, they are likely to take more control over their learning and to stay focused on their learning and progress. Opportunities to reflect on one's own work, discuss evaluation criteria, and set goals encourage students to think about their own thinking. For many third graders this type of metacognitive processing may be quite challenging. However, for fourth and especially fifth graders, it is an invaluable part of the learning process.

Children in Multi-Age Classrooms

The Guidelines and Checklists fit well in multi-age classrooms, defined as classrooms that combine students from at least two age or grade levels. Many of these classrooms use Guidelines and Checklists as their classroom assessment because of their emphasis on the continuum of children's development. By examining all six levels of an indicator presented in the Omnibus Guidelines, you can see what comes before and what comes after each indicator.

Teachers in multi-age classrooms face the challenge of creating curricular and instructional plans for a wide developmental range of students. Multi-age teachers using Guidelines and Checklists report that the Omnibus Guidelines help them understand how to modify curricular and instructional plans to accommodate differences in expectations for children at different ages. For example, knowing conventions of print is an important aspect of writing for all grade levels, but the Omnibus Guidelines show how expectations for this skill gradually change as children mature.

Although the Omnibus Guidelines present several levels of development at once, the Checklists do not. Teachers of multi-age groups use several different Checklists to reflect the developmental range their students represent. Thus, if you have a class of 7 and 8 year olds, you would complete second grade Checklists for the 7 year olds, and third grade Checklists for the 8 year olds. Because of the consistency of the domains, components, and many of the indicators across grade levels, you do not have to learn entirely new information for each age represented in your classroom. The rationales and examples describe the differences from one grade level to another. The Omnibus Guidelines supports your instructional planning by enabling you quickly to identify similarities and differences among age levels and to move easily between grade levels.

Children with Special Needs

The Work Sampling Guidelines and Checklists have been used successfully to assess children with special needs who are included in regular education classrooms. In fact, several features of the Checklist make it particularly appropriate for the assessment of children with special needs. First, it takes an individualized approach to learning and assessment. Children are not compared to one another, but are compared to standards of performance identified in the Developmental Guidelines. Moreover, because the Work Sampling Checklist evaluates progress as well as performance, it allows children with special needs to demonstrate growth even in areas where their performance is delayed.

Work Sampling's emphasis on ongoing assessment embedded within the classroom curriculum is also particularly relevant for children with special needs, many of whom have difficulty performing "on demand." In order to obtain an accurate picture of their strengths and weaknesses, it is critical to observe them over time and in a variety of circumstances. The emphasis Work Sampling places on repeated observation of learning within the classroom context ensures a comprehensive picture of each child's typical behavior.

Work Sampling's focus on classroom-based assessment and the use of assessment information to inform instruction makes it very compatible with the Individual Educational Plans (IEPs) required for children with special needs. IEPs provide detailed assessments of the child's needs and equally detailed plans for instruction that are updated regularly. Work Sampling's individualized profile of each child's development, created through extensive collection and observation of student work and behavior in seven domains, is a very useful and powerful method for informing the IEP. In addition, Work Sampling assists teachers in planning appropriate and meaningful curricula that promote the movement of children toward their greatest potential.

Many teachers have successfully linked the use of Work Sampling with IEPs. Figure 1 shows how one preschool teacher linked IEP language goals to Work Sampling performance indicators.

FIGURE 1

An Individual Education Plan (IEP) showing how IEP goals can be linked to Work Sampling performance indicators

---

Individual Education Plan

Student: _Tom_   Date of Birth: _5/14/94_   IEP From: _1/2/99_   To: _2/1/00_

Goals and Objectives   Domain: _Speech_   Sequence: _1.1_

Goal 1.1 – Tom will expand his expressive language, using language for a variety of purposes.

Objectives and Evaluation Procedure and Schedule

Objective 1.1.1 – Tom will be able to state how things are different when given a picture clue as well as when no clue is provided.
Evaluation Procedure: Classroom observation and informal testing
Evaluation Schedule: Semi-annual report June 99, annual review January 00

Objective 1.1.2 – Tom will demonstrate an understanding of prepositions (i.e., in, on, under, over, etc.).
Evaluation Procedure: Classroom observation and informal testing
Evaluation Schedule: Semi-annual report June 99, annual review January 00

Goals and Objectives   Domain: _Speech_   Sequence: _1.2_

Goal 1.2 – Tom will improve his speech sound production in order to speak clearly enough to be understood without contextual clues.

Objectives and Evaluation Procedure and Schedule

Objective 1.2.1 – Tom will correctly articulate the /th/ in the initial (think), medial (toothpaste) and final (with) positions in targeted and spontaneous speech.
Evaluation Procedure: Classroom observation and informal testing
Evaluation Schedule: Semi-annual report June 99, annual review January 00

Objective 1.2.2 – Tom will use -ing endings in targeted and spontaneous speech
Evaluation Procedure: Classroom observation and informal testing
Evaluation Schedule: Semi-annual report June 99, annual review January 00

Just as curricular adaptation may be necessary for a child with special needs to participate fully in learning activities, adaptations may also be needed in the Work Sampling Checklist. The severity of a child's handicapping condition will be a major determinant of the necessary adaptations. Modifications may include interpreting indicators in a more inclusive way, deleting certain indicators or components, and supplementing this assessment with other more specialized assessments.

In many places, it is possible to change the language of the performance indicators to encompass varied expressions of the indicator and the use of adaptive equipment. For example, in the domain of Language and Literacy, the first indicator under the component of Speaking in first grade is "Speaks clearly and conveys ideas effectively." "Speaking" can be interpreted as communicating in order to reflect the fact that some children with special needs may communicate in ways other than speaking (such as with gestures, signs, facial expressions, and communication boards). The language used in the Guidelines' indicators is designed to be inclusive so that a child's development can be noted even when a handicapping condition is present (for example, using the word "communicates" instead of "verbalizes" and "notices" instead of "sees").

Sometimes, particular indicators, components, or domains will assume greater importance for children with disabilities. For example, for children with physical impairments, learning how to ask for assistance and how to decline assistance appropriately are central to the development of independence. Similarly, the domain of Personal and Social Development assumes increased emphasis for children with behavioral or emotional disabilities.

Some components or performance indicators may not be appropriate for individual children and should be omitted. For example, most of the performance indicators in the Physical Development & Health section may not be appropriate for children with moderate to severe cerebral palsy. These indicators would be omitted and replaced with more relevant performance indicators or a different assessment. A third grade child with a moderate to severe mental impairment may require elimination of performance indicators requiring higher-level abstract thinking skills, such as "makes predictions based on data" in Scientific Thinking.

Obviously, limitations apply to the applicability of Work Sampling Checklists for some children with disabilities. Given the variety of needs even among children with the same disability, no single assessment can address all needs. Children with special needs may require additional assessment in some areas. For example, a child with motoric involvement may require intervention to improve oral-motor ability in order to help the child speak more clearly. In that case, a performance indicator could be added to encompass the area of oral-motor control. Similarly, a severe visual impairment warrants the assessment of mobility. When development in a given domain is very different or delayed, a specialized instrument administered by a therapist or special education consultant may be necessary to supplement information obtained through Work Sampling. When a child's functioning is below that of a three-year-old, other assessments would be more effective and informative than the Work Sampling Guidelines and Checklists.

Teachers frequently ask whether they should always use the Checklist that corresponds to a child's chronological age. This decision should be made in conjunction with family members and special education consultants. An important factor to consider is whether the child has a general developmental delay and is performing at a consistent level across the seven Work Sampling domains, or whether the child's performance varies widely from one domain to another. For example, if a child is experiencing a general developmental delay, using the grade level Checklist that corresponds to a child's chronological age may not be appropriate because all indicators would be rated "Not Yet." If all of the indicators are far beyond the child's current capabilities, then the Checklist would not demonstrate the child's progress, nor would it inform instructional planning. In such cases, it is more useful to use a Checklist that more nearly reflects the child's developmental age. In this way, the child's growth can be reflected as the year progresses.

In contrast, for children functioning near their age level in several domains, it may be most appropriate to use the Checklist that corresponds to their chronological age. This Checklist could be supplemented with additional assessments in areas of delay and with information from the Guidelines that describes younger children. However, it is important that teachers do not underestimate a child's capabilities by using a Checklist that most closely reflects the child's weakest area.

Working on a Team

We recommend that the classroom teacher collaborate with Special Education teachers and consultants. By using the child's Checklist, the teacher can communicate clearly with specialists and family members about how the child performs in the classroom. Because the classroom teacher spends more time with the child, she has a wealth of specific knowledge about how the child approaches learning. The rich, detailed, individualized portraits that the Work Sampling Checklist provides make it a valuable addition to the educational assessment of children with special needs.

Using Work Sampling for Title I Evaluation

Although the Work Sampling Guidelines and Checklists are primarily an instructional assessment that utilizes curriculum-embedded methods of record keeping and evaluation, they can be converted into Title I evaluations.

Translating Work Sampling Data into Title I Ratings

Checklists

To translate data from the Checklist into Title I terminology, the Checklist ratings are summarized *by domains* as follows:

WORK SAMPLING CHECKLIST	TITLE I
All ratings Proficient: student's work exceeds grade-level expectations	"Advanced"
Majority of ratings are Proficient with some In Process and no Not Yet ratings: student's work meets grade-level expectations	"Proficient"
Combination of Not Yet, In Process, and Proficient, or all In Process, or a combination of Not Yet and In Process ratings: student's work is inconsistent and does not meet grade-level expectations	"Partially Proficient"

Report To Parents

The ratings on the Work Sampling Report To Parents can be converted into Title I ratings as follows:

REPORT TO PARENTS	TITLE I
Advanced	"Advanced Proficient"
Proficient	"Proficient"
Partially Proficient **and** Needs Development	"Partially Proficient"

APPENDIX A

Glossary of Terms

Checklist—*see Developmental Checklist*

Checklist Ratings—*see In Process, Not Yet, Proficient*

Component—*see Functional Component*

Curriculum-embedded—an assessment that uses students' actual performance in the regular classroom routine as the "data" for evaluation.

Criterion-referenced—an assessment that evaluates a student's work with reference to specific criteria rather than with reference to other students' work.

Developmental Checklist—a list of performance indicators for each grade level that are organized by curriculum domains and are used to collect, organize, and record teachers' observations.

Developmental Guidelines—a book that describes age or grade level expectations for the performance indicators; contains a rationale and examples for each indicator.

Domain—a broad area of the curriculum.

Evaluation—consists of judging how closely something compares to a standard.

Examples—descriptions of ways that children demonstrate what they know and can do related to each performance indicator in the Developmental Guidelines.

Functional Component—a subset of a domain comprised of several performance indicators.

Guidelines—*see Developmental Guidelines*

Indicator—*see Performance Indicator*

In Process—a Checklist rating that indicates that the skill or knowledge represented by a performance indicator is intermittent or emergent, and is not demonstrated consistently.

Not Yet—a Checklist rating that indicates that a child cannot demonstrate the skill or knowledge represented by a performance indicator.

Observational Assessment—*see Curriculum-embedded*

Omnibus Guidelines—two volumes (P3–3, K–5) that each display six years of Developmental Guidelines on facing pages, arranged to show year-to-year progress.

Performance—refers to the level of a student's behavior, skills, and accomplishments at a particular point in time.

Performance Assessment—refers to assessment methods that rely on students demonstrating their knowledge or skills in applied situations.

Performance Indicator—a skill, behavior, attitude, or accomplishment that is evaluated in the classroom.

Proficient—a Checklist rating that indicates that the skill or knowledge represented by a performance indicator is demonstrated consistently, and is firmly within the child's repertoire.

Progress—growth over time.

Rationale—a brief explanation of an indicator that includes reasonable age or grade level expectations.

Reporting Period—a duration of time during which data are collected in an ongoing manner in order to make an evaluation. Work Sampling has three collection periods: fall, winter, and spring.

APPENDIX B

The Work Sampling Process Notes

The Work Sampling Process Notes provide teachers with a selection of optional forms to help record observation. They are designed to be used flexibly, allowing teachers to tailor their approach to best suit their needs and teaching styles. They are decribed on pages 32-36. The four forms are:

1 Domain Process Notes
2 Child Domain Process Notes
3 General Process Notes
4 Roster Process Notes

The forms and information in this book are subject to copyright. Pearson Early Learning hereby grants permission to the bearer to copy and use the forms in Appendix B as part of the bearer's use of the Work Sampling Guidelines and Checklists.

Page ____ of ____

Teacher ____

Domain Process Notes

I Personal & Social Development A Self concept B Self control C Approaches to learning D Interaction with others E Social problem-solving			
II Language & Literacy A Listening B Speaking C Reading D Writing E Research (3-5)			
III Mathematical Thinking A Mathematical processes B Number and operations C Patterns, relationships, and functions D Geometry and spatial relations E Measurement F Data collection & prob. (K-5)			
IV Scientific Thinking A Inquiry B Physical science (K-5) C Life science (K-5) D Earth science (K-5)			
V Social Studies A People, past and present B Human interdependence C Citizenship and government D People and where they live			
VI The Arts A Expression and representation B Understanding and appreciation			
VII Physical Development & Health A Gross motor development B Fine motor development C Personal health and safety			

Child Domain Process Notes

SPRING   WINTER   FALL   of   Page   Teacher

Child

I **Personal & Social Development**	II **Language & Literacy**
A Self concept	A Listening
B Self control	B Speaking
C Approaches to learning	C Reading
D Interaction with others	D Writing
E Social problem-solving	E Research (3-5)

III **Mathematical Thinking**	IV **Scientific Thinking**
A Mathematical processes	A Inquiry
B Number and operations	B Physical science (K-5)
C Patterns, relationships, and functions	C Life science (K-5)
D Geometry and spatial relations	D Earth science (K-5)
E Measurement	
F Data collection and probability (K-5)	

V **Social Studies**	VI **The Arts**
A People, past and present	A Expression and representation
B Human interdependence	B Understanding and appreciation
C Citizenship and government	
D People and where they live	

VII **Physical Development & Health**	Other Notes
A Gross motor development	
B Fine motor development	
C Personal health and safety	

Roster Process Notes	Teacher	Page	of	The Work Sampling System® © 2003 Pearson Education, Inc., publishing as Pearson Early Learning.						

Index

A

Anecdotal Notes **27, 47, 54**
    anecdotal records **39**
    extending knowledge of **20-23**
    how to observe and record **37-44**
    planning for **38-40**
    preparing methods and tools **23-37**

Assessment **1, 7, 21, 47**
    authentic performance assessment **1**
    curriculum-embedded **1**
    documentation **51**
    instructional assessment **2**
    introduction **7**
    observational **7**
    observational assessment **1**
    performance assessment **1, 2**
    role of context in **1, 21**
    student awareness of **43**

Audiotapes **30**

B

Binders **37**

Brief notes **27, 28, 34**

Butcher paper **32**

C

Calendars **31**

Carpenters' Aprons **32**

Checklist
    see also Guidelines, Observation, Documentation
    and children with special needs **80**
    as documentation **7**
    choosing appropriate age/grade level **53, 82**
    completing **6, 17**
    components **13**
    differences between reporting period **45, 51**
    domains **13**
    evaluating progress in **52**
    evaluation **7, 13**
    features **6**
    for planning curriculum and instruction **49, 60**
    how long to complete **53**
    how long to learn **53**
    in multi-age classrooms **79**
    in observation **7**
    in preschool **77**
    indicators **13**
    making final ratings **45, 47, 53**
    making preliminary ratings **40, 45-47**
    modifications in emphasis **77**
    overview **6**
    page reference of indicators to grade-level Guidelines **14**
    purposes of **8**
    ratings **13, 41, 59**
    reasons for three collection periods **52**
    reliability **50**
    reporting periods **13**
    reviewing periodically **40**
    reviewing to plan observation **38, 44**
    sharing the Checklist with families **52**
    space for written comments **14, 42**
    specialists **55**
    status at year-end **52**
    storage **36**
    student involvement in **42**
    student's identifying information **14**
    translating data to Title I ratings **84**
    using **6, 17**
    using Guidelines as reference **45**
    validity **50**
    Wall Chart of Performance Indicators **20, 42**
    when to complete **17**

Checklist ratings, See Checklist

CHILD DOMAIN PROCESS NOTES **33**

Child Involvement, See Student Involvement

Children, See Students

Comments on Work Sampling Report **69**
    audience **70**
    content **70**
    how much to write **71**
    issues **70**
    language **71**
    purpose **70**

COMPONENTS
    on the Checklist **9, 14**
    definition **10**
    in grade-level Guidelines **11, 13**
    in the Omnibus Guidelines **9, 16**
    relation to domains **12**
    relation to indicators **12**
    variation in different age/grade levels **11**

Computers, hand-held **32**

Conferences with Families
    See also Family Involvement, Student Involvement
    preparing for **73**
    student involvement in **73**
    student-led conferences **74**

Criterion-Referenced, See Guidelines

Curriculum-Embedded Assessment, See Assessment

D

DEVELOPMENTAL CHECKLIST **13**

Developmental Checklist, See Checklist

Developmental Guidelines, See Guidelines

Documentation
    See also Documentation Methods and Tools, Observation, Storage
    Checklist as **7**
    difference between fact and opinion **22**
    difference between informal and formal records **51**
    Domain Process Notes form **32, 35**
    establishing realistic expectations **24, 47**
    for planning curriculum and instruction **49**
    General Process Notes form **34, 36**
    how to observe and record **37-44**
    in assessment **51**
    including opinions in **22**
    managing **47, 54**
    methods **26-30**
    of multiple indicators **54**
    of observation while participating in the action **23**
    of observations after the fact **25**

Index

Index